Creating a
Culture of
LIFE

Creating a Culture of LIFE

KENNETH R. OVERBERG, S.J.

ThomasMore®
– An RCL Company –

Allen, Texas

NIHIL OBSTAT:
Rev. Msgr. Glenn D. Gardner, J.C.D.
Censor Librorum

IMPRIMATUR:
† Most Rev. Charles V. Grahmann
Bishop of Dallas

March 15, 2002

The Nihil Obstat and Imprimatur are official declarations that the material reviewed is free of doctrinal or moral error. No implication is contained therein that those granting the Nihil Obstat and Imprimatur agree with the contents, opinions, or statements expressed.

Acknowledgment
Quotations from *Vatican Council II: The Basic Sixteen Documents* (in inclusive language), Austin Flannery, P.P., general editor, Costello Publishing and Dominican Publications, 1996.

The Scripture quotations contained herein are from the *New Revised Standard Version Bible: Catholic Edition* copyright © 1993 and 1989 by the Division of Christian Education for the National Council of the Churches of Christ in the U.S.A. Used by permission. All rights reserved.

Some material in this book previously appeared in the *Catholic Telegraph* and *Catholic Update*.

Send all inquiries to:
Thomas More® Publishing
An RCL Company
200 East Bethany Drive
Allen, Texas 75002-3804

Telephone: 800-264-0368 / 972-390-6300
Fax: 800-688-8356 / 972-390-6560

Visit us at: **www.thomasmore.com**
Customer Service E-mail: **cservice@rcl-enterprises.com**

Printed in the United States of America

Library of Congress Control Number: 2002102194

7487   ISBN 0-88347-487-5

1 2 3 4 5   06 05 04 03 02

Dedication

To all those who nourish life,
with special thoughts of my family and friends

Contents

Preface

S ome years ago I participated in a study tour to the lands of the Bible. To avoid the heat of the day, our group climbed Mt. Sinai during the night along a steep, winding path. Just before the final part of the climb (700 rock steps) there is a stone bench. While most of the group turned the bend in the path to climb the steps, a few of us waited on the bench for sunrise.

In the quiet, we prayerfully read the first chapters of Genesis. Gradually the sun appeared (cover photo). The combination of God's word and awesome beauty produced in me a sense of being present at creation.

Literally and symbolically, this moment was a peak experience. We cannot live on the mountaintop, however, either when on pilgrimage or in our everyday lives. Still, as God's people we are called to continue God's work, to be co-creators. In our time, an especially challenging task is to help create a culture of life.

The essays in this book offer some musings on living the consistent ethic of life throughout our lives and in all dimensions of our lives. A quotation from Vatican II's *Pastoral Constitution on the Church in the Modern World* sets the context for each of the five groups of essays, reminding us of not only that great council's desire for the renewal of moral theology but also its inspiring vision of authentic Christian living. *Creating a Culture of Life* will be helpful for private pondering and prayer, for small faith-group discussions, for anyone looking for a gentle introduction to Catholic morality.

A wonderful prayerful reflection, popularly attributed to Archbishop Oscar Romero, describes well the purpose of and my hopes for this little book:

It helps now and then to step back and take the long view. The kingdom is not only beyond our efforts, it is even beyond our vision. We accomplish in our lifetime only a tiny fraction of the magnificent enterprise that is God's work. Nothing we do is complete, which is another way of saying that the kingdom always lies beyond us.

No statement says all that should be said. No prayer fully expresses our faith. No confession brings perfection. No pastoral visit brings wholeness. No program accomplishes the church's mission. No set of goals and objectives includes everything.

This is what we are about: we plant the seeds that one day will grow. We water seeds already planted, knowing that they hold future promise. We lay foundations that will need further development. We provide yeast that produces effects far beyond our capabilities.

We cannot do everything, and there is a sense of liberation in realizing that. This enables us to do something, and to do it very well. It may be incomplete, but it is a beginning, a step along the way, an opportunity for the Lord's grace to enter and do the rest.

We may never see the end results, but that is the difference between the master builder and the worker. We are workers, not master builders; ministers, not messiahs. We are prophets of a future that is not our own.

Finally, I want to express my gratitude to Tricia Hempel, Dennis O'Connor, John Bookser Feister, and Jack Wintz, O.F.M., for their encouragement and support of my work. Special thanks to Darleen Frickman, the secretary for Xavier University's theology department, for all her fine work, including the many details connected with this book. Also special thanks to Arthur J. Dewey, wordsmith and scholar, colleague and friend.

PART I

A Consistent Ethic of Life

*The people of God believes that it is led by the Spirit
of the Lord who fills the whole world. Impelled by that faith,
they try to discern the true signs of God's presence and purpose
in the events, the needs and the desires which it shares with
the rest of humanity today. For faith casts a new light
on everything and makes known the full ideal which God
has set for humanity, thus guiding the mind towards
solutions that are fully human.*

*[A]ll offenses against life itself, such as murder, genocide,
abortion, euthanasia and willful suicide; all violations
of the integrity of the human person, such as . . . physical
and mental torture . . . ; all offenses against human dignity,
such as subhuman living conditions . . . the selling of women
and children, degrading working conditions . . . all these
and the like are criminal: they poison civilization;
and they debase the perpetrators more than the victims
and militate against the honor of the creator.*

Pastoral Constitution on the Church in the Modern World, 11, 27

1

Choosing Life
from Womb to Tomb

We are all too aware of the darkness in our lives, in our world. Violence of all kinds threatens life: in our homes, in our cities, in nations near and far. "Violence has many faces: oppression of the poor, deprivation of basic human rights, economic exploitation, sexual exploitation and pornography, neglect or abuse of the aged and the helpless, and innumerable other acts of inhumanity. Abortion in particular blunts a sense of the sacredness of human life."

We see this passage from the American bishops' pastoral letter on peace exemplified almost every day in the headlines. Many of us have directly encountered some form of violence in our own lives. Many more of us suffer with families and friends. How can we respond to this violence and death?

A moral vision that holds together these many different issues and offers not only direction for action but also energy and hope is the consistent ethic of life. The late Cardinal Joseph Bernardin articulated this perspective in the early 1980s, and it has become a centerpiece of the American Catholic bishops' moral teaching. Pope John Paul II has affirmed similar themes in his 1995 encyclical *The Gospel of Life*. These sources answer the three basic questions: (1) What is the consistent ethic of life? (2) Where does it come from? (3) What does it mean for our everyday lives?

A MORAL FRAMEWORK

What is the consistent ethic of life? It is a comprehensive ethical system that links together many different issues by focusing attention on the basic value of life. In his attempts to defend life, Cardinal Bernardin first joined the topics of abortion and nuclear war. He quickly expanded his understanding of a consistent ethic of life to include many issues from all of life. Already in the first of a whole series of talks, Cardinal Bernardin stated: "The spectrum of life cuts across the issues of genetics, abortion, capital punishment, modern warfare and the care of the terminally ill" (Fordham address).

Cardinal Bernardin also acknowledged that issues are distinct and different; capital punishment, for example, is not the same as abortion. Nevertheless, the issues are linked. The valuing and defense of life is at the center of both issues. Cardinal Bernardin wrote: "When human life is considered 'cheap' or easily expendable in one area, eventually nothing is held as sacred and all lives are in jeopardy" (Portland address).

Along with his consistent linking of distinct life issues, Cardinal Bernardin acknowledged that no individual or

LINKING LIFE ISSUES

If one contends, as we do, that the right of every fetus to be born should be protected by civil law and supported by civil consensus, then our moral, political and economic responsibilities do not stop at the moment of birth. Those who defend the right to life of the weakest among us must be equally visible in support of the quality of life of the powerless among us: the old and the young, the hungry and the homeless, the undocumented immigrant and the unemployed worker. Such a quality of life posture translates into specific political and economic positions on tax policy, employment generation, welfare policy, nutrition and feeding programs, and health care.

—Cardinal Joseph Bernardin
(*Consistent Ethic of Life*, Sheed & Ward)

group can pursue all issues. Still, while concentrating on one issue, the individual or group must not be seen "as insensitive to or even opposed to other moral claims on the overall spectrum of life" (St. Louis address). The consistent ethic of life rules out contradictory moral positions about the unique value of human life—and it would be contradictory, for example, to be against abortion but for capital punishment or to work against poverty but support euthanasia.

This linkage of all life issues is, of course, the very heart of the consistent ethic of life. This linkage challenges us to move beyond the contradictions we may find in our own convictions about morality. Often these convictions seem to cluster around "conservative" or "liberal" viewpoints—as in the above examples. But the consistent ethic of life cuts across such divisions, calling us to respect the life in the womb, the life of a criminal, the life on welfare, the life of the dying.

SOURCES OF LIFE

Where does the consistent ethic of life come from? Recent sources include the addresses and articles of Cardinal Bernardin, the teachings of the American Catholic bishops, and John Paul II's encyclical *The Gospel of Life*. The ultimate source, however, is the Bible, especially the life and teaching of Jesus.

Cardinal Bernardin, because of his extensive experience in the work of the National Conference of Catholic Bishops, spent much time and energy on two issues: abortion and nuclear war. He found committed people concerned about one issue but not the other. As he worked to bring together those seeking an end to abortion and those trying to prevent nuclear war, Cardinal Bernardin began to emphasize the linkage among the life issues. This emphasis has been continued in the teachings of the National Conference of Catholic Bishops.

Pope John Paul II's encyclical *The Gospel of Life* is another bold and prophetic defense of life. Although it does not use the phrase, *The Gospel of Life* strongly affirms the consistent ethic of life. John Paul describes what is going on in our world today: a monumental

15

abuse of life through drugs, war and arms, abortion, euthanasia, destruction of the environment, unjust distribution of resources. This abuse is often caused and supported by the economic, social, and political structures of the nations. So the pope speaks of a "structure of sin" and a "culture of death" and a "conspiracy against life" (*The Gospel of Life,* 12).

The pope also proclaims the Christian understanding of the value of life. Created in God's image, redeemed by Jesus, called to everlasting life, every human being is sacred and social; every human being is a sign of God's love. In much more detail than Cardinal Bernardin's addresses, the pope provides the foundation for building a culture of life by weaving together a wealth of biblical texts which clearly proclaim human dignity.

The consistent ethic of life is ultimately rooted in Jesus, in whom the meaning and value of life are definitively proclaimed and fully given. John Paul II states this insight with these words: "*The Gospel of life* is not simply a reflection, however new and profound, on human life. Nor is it merely a commandment aimed at raising awareness and bringing about significant changes in society. Still less is it an illusory promise of a better future. *The Gospel of life* is something concrete and personal, for it consists in the proclamation of *the very person of Jesus*" (29).

Who is this Jesus? We have to be careful not to create Jesus in our own image. As Scripture scholar John Meier reminds us, Jesus was a "nonconformist" who associated with the religious and social outcasts. As a result of his life and teachings, Jesus "escapes all our neat categories" and is neither right nor left (see "Jesus" in *The New Jerome Biblical Commentary,* Prentice Hall, 1990, 1968). This is the Jesus of the Sermon on the Mount who proclaims as blessed not the leaders of society but the mourning and the meek, the poor and the pure, the persecuted and the peacemaker (Matthew 5:1–12). This is the Jesus who praises not power but reconciliation in the story about the forgiving father of the prodigal son (Luke 15:11–32). This is the Jesus of faithful ministry, of suffering and death, of new life

(Mark 14:3–16:8). This is the Jesus who says, "I came that they may have life, and have it abundantly" (John 10:10). Who Jesus is and what Jesus means by abundant life, then, are surely different from what the consumerism and individualism of our culture tell us about life.

ABUNDANT LIFE

What does the consistent ethic of life mean for our everyday lives? (1) It encourages us to hold together a great variety of issues with a consistent focus on the value of life. (2) It challenges us to reflect on our basic values and convictions which give direction to our lives. (3) It leads us to express our commitment to life in civil debate and public policy.

From Womb to Tomb

A consistent ethic includes all life issues from the very beginning of life to its end. An excellent example of how the life ethic holds together many distinct issues is the American bishops' statement *Political Responsibility*, issued prior to every presidential election. The 1996 edition of *Political Responsibility* provided direction concerning many issues, including abortion, racism, the economy, AIDS, housing, the global trade in arms, welfare reform, immigration, and refugees.

Several examples can give the spirit of *Political Responsibility* and help us examine our consciences. The bishops oppose the use of the death penalty, judging that the practice further undermines respect for life in our society and stating that it has been discriminatory against the poor and racial minorities. The bishops express special concern for the problem of racism, calling it a "radical evil" which divides the human family. Dealing with poverty, the bishops claim, is a moral imperative of the highest priority, for poverty threatens life. In the domestic scene, there is a need for more jobs with adequate pay and decent working conditions; at the international level, the areas of trade, aid, and investment must be reevaluated

17

in terms of their impact on the poor.

Racism, poverty, capital punishment—certainly these are very different issues, with different causes and different solutions (many of which may be very complex). Still, underneath all these differences is life and, for us, the challenge of respecting the lives of people who may be very different from us. What actions concerning these issues would a consistent ethic of life suggest? Here are a few possibilities: For capital punishment, spend time learning why many churches are opposed to the death penalty; then write to your governor and other officials expressing your opposition. For racism, start or join a parish group that is working to bring together people of different races (perhaps by "twinning" parishes). For poverty, read the bishops' pastoral letter *Economic Justice for All* (1986); volunteer in a soup kitchen or an AIDS clinic; if possible, exercise your leadership in business or politics to change oppressive policies and regulations. Surely, we cannot do everything; but we can do one thing.

> *We stand with the unborn and the undocumented when many politicians seem to be abandoning them. We defend children in the womb and on welfare. We oppose the violence of abortion and the vengeance of capital punishment.*
>
> —Political Responsibility: Proclaiming the Gospel of Life, Protecting the Least Among Us, and Pursuing the Common Good

A Question of Values

The consistent ethic of life also leads us beyond the specific issues to the depths of our convictions about the meaning of life. A careful and prayerful study of *Political Responsibility* (and the more detailed teachings which it summarizes) allows us to appreciate not only the expanse of the seamless garment of the consistent ethic of life but also its profound challenge to our most important attitudes and values.

Emphasizing the consistent ethic of life and recognizing its countercultural directions, the bishops state: "Our moral framework does not easily fit the categories of right or left, Republican or Democrat. We are called to measure every party and movement by how its agenda touches human life and human dignity." It is not sufficient to be pro-life on some issues; we must be pro-life on all issues—no matter what our political party or business or union or talk shows or advertising or family may say. These are powerful forces which significantly shape our convictions. They often lead to the contradictions which separate us from a consistent ethic of life. Politics, media, money, and class—and not our faith—may well be the real source of our values.

We ought not underestimate the challenge of being pro-life; it is so easy to justify our contradictions by appealing to common sense or accepted business practice or the ethical relativism which is our culture's morality. In *The Gospel of Life* John Paul II urges all persons to choose life—consistently, personally, nationally, globally. This invitation is really a profound challenge: to look deeply into ourselves and to test against the Gospel some of our own deeply held beliefs and practices. John Paul writes: "In a word, we can say that the cultural change which we are calling for demands from everyone the courage to *adopt a new lifestyle*, consisting in making practical choices—at the personal, family, social and international level—on the basis of a correct scale of values: *the primacy of being over having, of the person over things*. This renewed lifestyle involves a passing from *indifference to concern for others, from rejection to acceptance of them*" (*The Gospel of Life*, 98).

Public Policy

Cardinal Bernardin, the conference of bishops, and Pope John Paul have necessarily discussed the relationship between moral vision and political policies. Indeed, the consistent ethic of life was developed to help shape public policy. Political policies and economic structures provide means to create a societal environment that promotes the flourishing of human life. During the past one hundred years, bishops and popes have addressed these very issues in their social teachings.

As Cardinal Bernardin realized, we must also be able to state our case "in nonreligious terms which others of different faith convictions might find morally persuasive" (Fordham address). For example, we may be opposed to euthanasia and assisted suicide fundamentally because of our faith convictions about God as giver of the gift of life and about our own stewardship of life. For public policy discussion, however, we may stress other reasons, such as human dignity, the undermining of trust in the medical profession, the threat to women and the vulnerable.

Political Responsibility and *The Gospel of Life* emphasize that faithfulness to the Gospel leads not only to individual acts of charity but also to actions involving the institutions and structures of society, the economy, and politics. The American bishops, for example, state: "We encourage people to use their voices and votes to enrich the democratic life of our nation and to act on their values in the political arena. We hope American Catholics, as both believers *and* citizens, will use the resources of our faith and the opportunities of this democracy to help shape a society more respectful of the life, dignity, and rights of the human person, especially the poor and vulnerable." Clearly, religion and politics must mix in our lives! We face the challenge of embodying consistently an ethic of life in the candidates we support and in our own direct involvement in forming public policy (whether that be in the Girl Scouts or in a parish committee or in a local school board or in the U.S. Congress).

> *I*n *confronting a culture of violence, our Church calls for . . . attacking the root causes of violence, including poverty, substance abuse, lack of opportunity, racism, and family disintegration.*
>
> *—Political Responsibility: Proclaiming the Gospel of Life, Protecting the Least Among Us, and Pursuing the Common Good*

THE CHALLENGE OF DISCIPLESHIP

As we enter a new millennium, world events and church teachings direct our attention to life itself as the very center of our concern. The consistent ethic of life provides both a solid foundation and a powerful challenge to live as faithful disciples and involved citizens. It calls into question all views that contradict the message and meaning of Jesus. It challenges us to reject the culture of death and to create a culture of life in and through our everyday activities at home and at work and in society. How? The way we vote, the jokes we tell, the language we use, the attitudes we hand on to children, the causes we support, the business practices we use, the entertainment we attend, the way we care for the sick and elderly: in all these ordinary activities we express consistency in respecting life or we get trapped in contradictions.

The consistent ethic of life urges us to speak and act concerning abortion and euthanasia but also concerning welfare and immigration, sexism and racism, cloning and health-care reform, trade agreements and sweatshops, the buying and selling of women for prostitution, genocide, and many other issues. Based on our ancient Scriptures and attentive to contemporary experiences, the consistent ethic of life provides an ethical framework for confronting the moral dilemmas of a new millennium and for promoting the full flourishing of all life.

QUESTION BOX

1. What are your basic values and where do they come from?
2. Can you praise the good in the American way of life but also honestly acknowledge how it is a culture of death? In what ways?
3. What concrete action can you do to embody your commitment to a consistent ethic of life?

2

Moral Theology and Truth

E veryday headlines jar us with news about profound ethical issues. Genocide, racism, hunger, abortion, sexism: again and again we hear of tragic situations and violent actions. Some cases may seem overwhelming yet distant—what can I do about the war in some distant country? Others may be very close to home—what kind of treatment is morally right for my dying grandmother?

All of us face moral dilemmas. Our moral choices are significant because they shape the kind of person we are becoming, because they impact the lives of other people, because they nurture or damage our relationship with God.

In this book, I will muse with you about the moral dilemmas of our day. What exactly are the issues? What is our—and the human community's—experience? What light and guidance does the Christian tradition offer us? What ought we to do?

What is probably the most important issue, however, usually does not make headlines. It is the *way* we make our choices, the process of moral decision making. And at the heart of this issue is the ancient question, expressed perfectly by Pilate: "What is truth?"

Some would answer that each person must decide for himself or herself. This view is certainly popular in the United States, with its emphasis on individual rights. Indeed, most if not all of us have been deeply influenced by individualism simply by living in our culture. Pope John Paul II raised serious concerns about this relativism in his encyclical *The Splendor of Truth* (1993).

Other people argue that some authority—whether Jesus or the pope or Scripture—decides what is right, and so we must follow the law. Those of us who grew up in a pre-Vatican II Church know this view well. Yet we also know that sometimes the letter of the law oppresses the spirit or simply cannot deal with the complexity of a particular case.

The Roman Catholic tradition, recognizing the values and limits in both of these approaches, developed a third view. After careful discernment the individual must decide, but always in the context of the community's wisdom and with an understanding of what is really happening—not what we would like to happen. There is a certain objectivity to our actions; they have real meanings and consequences.

Truth, then, is not simply what I say it is, but what *we,* the human community with the help of God's revelation, discover it to be. Morality, what we ought to do to be truly human, is based on this truth. For example, humanity recognized that killing another human being is evil, that this action not only takes another's life but also seriously damages the spirit of the killer. We discover a truth about human life, which then shapes our morality.

So much more must be said, must be nuanced. If you feel impatient that we have not yet arrived at one of those emotional and controversial topics, remember that we will—but also that the process of deciding is of great importance. So, in the meantime, how do *you* answer Pilate's question?

3

Conscience

"**I** must follow my conscience!" Most of us have heard and probably used this bold declaration. More than a few times we hear it in the context of not following a particular law.

"I must follow my conscience." Of course. This statement is a sound principle—*if* it is properly understood.

Before we look at a careful description of conscience, let's first set the context. In my last essay, I described how the human community discovers truth. The harsh reality, however, is that the human community rarely acts in a unified way. Indeed, we find ourselves existing as part of a number of communities, each with its own values and commitments. For example, we are part of Christianity, with its Scriptures providing the basis for our convictions. But we are also part of early twenty-first century American culture, with its consumerism and materialism expressed by TV, movies, and advertising. Often the values of these two different communities are in profound conflict. We must choose which community will be our "home," which values direct our lives—even as we acknowledge that we compromise at times.

In this context of conflicting values, we find ourselves and take a stand. We can show the reasonableness of our choice, but never prove it. In this context, conscience is formed, a process which is a lifelong task. Conscience is not a little voice inside us telling us what to do. It is not a computer program inserted into us; nor is it an inner police officer or parent tapes. Conscience is my most personal self trying to make sound judgments about moral questions.

In his book *Principles for a Catholic Morality,* Timothy O'Connell has succinctly summarized the Christian tradition's understanding of conscience, describing it as three dimensions of the self: (1) general moral awareness, (2) the search for truth, (3) the concrete judgment.

The first dimension of conscience is the general sense of value which is characteristic of human beings. We are aware that we should do good and avoid evil.

The second dimension of conscience is the search to discover what really is the right course of action. If we are honest in our search, then we will consult a variety of sources for wisdom and guidance: Scripture, the Church, the sciences, competent professionals, etc. This "formation of conscience" is where the guidance of authority is especially helpful. Here also is where the conflict of competing communities is especially acute.

The third dimension of conscience is the actual concrete judgment. After searching for the truth, an individual reaches the point when a specific decision must be made.

This is when we say, "I must follow my conscience." Something very important is presupposed here: I must follow my decision (third dimension) *only* after I have done my best in discovering the truth (second dimension). Following my conscience does not mean doing what I feel like doing. It means doing the hard work of discerning what is right and what is wrong.

Are you willing to do this hard work that is part of a mature morality?

4

Images of God

Relationship with God is the heart of our moral life. The images we have of God play an important role in how this relationship develops. If, as we grew up, we were taught about a God who judges and punishes us, then our relationship might be characterized by fear or even avoidance. If, instead, God's love and forgiveness had been emphasized, we probably have a very different relationship with God.

The Eucharist and other sacraments and private prayer continue to influence our images of God and so shape our relationship. Other experiences, past and present, also influence how we think and feel about God, for example, if we had an abusive father or if we have experienced a deep and almost unconditional love.

One summer at the Jesuit Retreat House in Gloucester, Massachusetts, I had the opportunity to reflect on images of God. The natural setting is very conducive to prayer. The building faces a quiet cove with a small beach and the property extends to the ocean itself. There the surf pounds against massive mounds and blocks of granite. This wide expanse of granite provides lots of places for walking, climbing, and just sitting and pondering the immensity of the ocean—and the age and firmness of the granite itself. Geologists say that the granite is many millions of years old—now that puts perspective on everyday problems and musings!

Standing on this ancient granite reminded me of the Scriptural image of God as ROCK. Listen to the psalmist: "I love you, O LORD, my strength. The LORD is my rock, my fortress, and my deliverer, my

God, my rock in whom I take refuge" (Psalm 18:1–2). "[God] alone is my rock and my salvation, my fortress; I shall never be shaken" (Psalm 62:2). Hardly an image of tenderness or compassion or any other personal quality. Yet the psalmist is comfortable calling God a rock.

A wise Scripture scholar once said that we need to *multiply* our images of God. Different images help us to appreciate different aspects of God, who is always greater than any one description. But each image can give us a glimpse of the Holy Mystery, the source and goal of all life, and so nurture our relationship with God.

Unfortunately, in the church today people often debate or bitterly quarrel over various images of God. Yet the Bible itself offers us a wonderful variety, including fire, love, shepherd, warrior, shelter, light, bread of life, the Holy One. Deuteronomy, Second Isaiah (chapters 40–55 of the Book of Isaiah), and Wisdom all speak of God in maternal terms (see Deuteronomy 32:18 and Isaiah 46:3–4, for example). Hosea describes God as a gentle parent (11:1–4). Jesus calls God *Abba* ("Daddy"), and his parables point to an intimate, loving relationship with a merciful and faithful God (see Luke 15:11–32, for example).

What image of God is at the root of your relationship with God? What new images of God would enrich this relationship—and your moral life?

5

Jesus and the Consistent Ethic of Life

"The nonconformist Jesus who associated with the religious and social 'lowlife' of Palestine also serves as a corrective to a Christianity that is ever tempted to become respectable by this world's standards. . . . The fact is that the historical Jesus escapes all our neat categories and programs. . . . While at first glance attractively relevant, the historical Jesus will always strike the careful inquirer as strange, disturbing, even offensive. . . . He frustrates all attempts to turn Christian faith into relevant ideology, right or left, and is a constant catalyst for renewing theological thought and church life" (from "Jesus" by noted Scripture scholar John P. Meier, in *The New Jerome Biblical Commentary,* Prentice Hall, 1990, 1968).

Challenging words, aren't they? At least if we take them seriously and apply them to our lives.

If Jesus escapes all neat categories and is neither right nor left, then faithful disciples of Jesus can expect to be similar to the One they follow. But it is so hard for us to take in and live Gospel values. We receive so many messages which contradict the Gospel—powerful messages from advertising, political parties, TV and films, newspapers, business, even our families. Our understanding of the meaning of life and our reactions to events in our world often are rooted in these competing messages rather than in our Scriptures.

In an attempt to express Gospel values in our society, Cardinal Joseph Bernardin focused on a "consistent ethic of life." This theme has become a centerpiece of the teachings of the American Catholic bishops, and I will come back to it often. The consistent ethic of life is neither right nor left, neither Republican nor Democratic. Recognizing the dignity and sanctity of life from womb to tomb, it challenges all views that contradict the message and meaning of Jesus.

Shortly before his death, Cardinal Bernardin wrote: "It is easy in the rush of daily life or in its tedium to lose the sense of wonder that is appropriate to this gift [of human life]. It is even easier at the level of our societal relations to count some lives as less valuable than others, especially when caring for them costs us—financially, emotionally, or in terms of time, effort and struggle" (*America*, October 5, 1996).

Recent years provide many examples of the conflict between the consistent ethic of life and some of our own deeply held convictions (rooted in those "other" messages): the partial-birth abortion and assisted suicide debates, with their emphasis on privacy and individual choice; the Timothy McVeigh trial and the death penalty in general, with the emphasis on revenge and retribution; the welfare and immigration discussions, with their emphasis on the restriction of services and benefits. The list goes on and on. Cloning, hunger, war, domestic violence, racism—all have been in the headlines and all call us to find concrete ways to embody a consistent ethic of life.

What steps can you take to move beyond competing political or economic or cultural convictions to embrace a consistent ethic of life?

~ **PART II** ~

Following Jesus
Through the Year

The Word of God, through whom all things were made,
was made flesh, so that as a perfect man he could save
all women and men and sum up all things in himself.
The Lord is the goal of human history, the focal point
of the desires of history and civilization, the center of
humanity, the joy of all hearts, and the fulfillment of all
aspirations. It is he whom the Father raised from the dead,
exalted and placed at his right hand, constituting him judge
of the living and the dead. Animated and drawn together
in his Spirit we press onwards on our journey towards
the consummation of history which fully corresponds
to the plan of his love: "to unite all things in him,
things in heaven and things on earth" (Ephesians 1:10).

Pastoral Constitution on the Church in the Modern World, 45

6

Christmas and a Culture of Life

In our northern hemisphere, Christmas reflects the season. Though winter is officially just starting, its darkness already begins to give way to the promise of spring. Gradually we begin to experience more and more light. What an appropriate time to proclaim Jesus as Emmanuel, "God with us," who is light for our life's journey! Our celebration of the birth of Jesus is also a wonderful time to reflect on the gift of life.

Light and life—marvelous gifts, profound symbols, and great challenges. The prologue of John's Gospel, which is the gospel for Christmas Day, uses these symbols to guide our meditation on these gifts and challenges. John's sweeping vision begins with creation and moves forward to the Incarnation. In the beginning was the Word, and all things came to be through the Word. The Word became flesh and pitched his tent among us. This light shines in the darkness, and the darkness has not overcome it.

What a magnificent statement about God's creative and faithful love! We have so many reasons to be thankful and to trust. But sober realism also marks John's opening vision: there is darkness; the world did not know the Word; people did not accept him.

We are all too aware of the darkness in our lives, in our world. Violence of all kinds threatens life: in our homes, in our cities, in nations near and far. Especially at Christmastime, we are overwhelmed with the "gospel" of our consumer society. Advertising tries to convince us that our identity and value are found in the things we possess—in clothes and cars and perfume. Failing to find true meaning, we numb ourselves with alcohol and other drugs. In the words of Pope John Paul II, we live in a "culture of death."

Our challenges, then, are great: to live as faithful disciples of Jesus when so much in our society offers an opposite ideal; to work to create a "culture of life" in our communities and nation. As I mentioned in chapter 1, Cardinal Bernardin offered us some guidance in his lectures on the consistent ethic of life and Pope John Paul II emphasized this connecting of life issues in his encyclical *The Gospel of Life*. From womb to tomb we must care for life.

Such caring necessarily involves economic, cultural, and political decisions—all with profound religious implications. Unfortunately, in our society no one political party can fully help us in creating a "culture of life." In different ways both Republicans and Democrats dramatically fail to respect and promote life. The statement of the U.S. bishops on "Political Responsibility" clearly demonstrates this sad conclusion.

So, our challenges are great: to reflect on, pray over, and embody the Gospel of Life; to share our values and convictions with others; to find concrete ways to change death-dealing structures of our society.

Still, we can be people of hope. God is with us. "The light shines in the darkness, and the darkness has not overcome it." Do you dare to believe and live this bold proclamation?

~ 7 ~

Joseph and the Spiritual Life

O n March 19 the Church celebrates the feast of Saint Joseph.
Although there are many legends about Joseph, we actually
know very little about him. Even the stories in the Gospels are influenced by their major theological purpose, proclaiming the full
identity of Jesus. Still, remembering and celebrating Joseph can
surely deepen our moral-spiritual lives.

First, let's turn to Matthew's Gospel. In describing the birth of
Jesus, Matthew tells how Joseph dealt with a disturbing situation.
"When [Jesus'] mother Mary had been engaged to Joseph, but before
they lived together, she was found to be with child from the Holy
Spirit. Her husband Joseph, being a righteous man and unwilling to
expose her to public disgrace, planned to dismiss her quietly"
(Matthew 1:18–19).

Joseph was a "righteous man"—that is, a devout observer of the
Mosaic law—yet he decided not to follow the letter of the law. Mary
could have been shamed by a public trial or even stoned to death
(see Deuteronomy 22:21–23). But Matthew says Joseph decided
simply to dismiss Mary quietly. Only then does Matthew describe
Joseph's dream in which the angel of the Lord "explained" the whole
situation to Joseph (Matthew 1:20–23).

Matthew's story is, of course, a symbolic account. Still, the
insight remains: the righteous one was able to discern when not to
follow the letter of the law. (I am grateful to a member of my Jesuit
community who shared this interpretation of the passage with us as
we prayed about this scene.) Laws are very important guides for our

actions, and so must be taken seriously. But we must also be attentive to the spirit of the law and to the Holy Spirit leading us as we face complex moral dilemmas. This emphasis surely does *not* imply an ethical relativism, but does stress the importance of prayerful discernment.

The second insight concerning Joseph is only a reasonable guess. In the Scriptures, Jesus often addresses God as Father, even *Abba*, which is best translated "Daddy." The expression points to a very intimate, loving relationship between God and Jesus—and perhaps, along with "kingdom" language, to a new political model.

What about Joseph? As Jesus grew up, he must have had a wonderful father. What better way for Jesus to come to know with deep conviction who a good "daddy" is and how he acts! Joseph must have been an image of God for Jesus. Later, in his teachings and prayers and parables (see especially Luke 15:11–32), Jesus speaks of a God who is forgiving, loving, compassionate, and gentle.

Today we know that many people have the opposite experience—because of suffering from an abusive father, they find it difficult to pray to God as Father. Surely, healing is needed here; other images of God may be more appropriate for prayer. We also know that God is neither male nor female, but personal images are helpful in our relating to God. For Jesus, the image of daddy seems to have been a special one—and Joseph may have played an important part in building the foundation of that image.

How will your remembering and celebrating Joseph deepen and renew your moral-spiritual life?

8

Lenten Lament

"O LORD, I cry out to you. I am desperate." For most if not all of us, there are times in our lives when we want to join the psalmist in crying out to God, expressing our despair and anger. Yet, we may hesitate, somehow sensing that we ought not address God in this way.

Fortunately, our Scriptures are rich in lament, teaching us that it is not only good but necessary to cry out to God. See, for example, the books of Job and Lamentations, and also many of the Psalms, including 39, 44, 53, 77, 88, 89, 106, 109, 143. Biblical scholars have helped us to appreciate what these laments meant to the people of God then (see *The Catholic Study Bible*, for example) and what they can mean for us today.

Lament marked the very beginning of the history of the Hebrew people—and so the beginning of our religious story too. In their oppression the people cried out to God, and God heard and acted, leading them to freedom (see Exodus 2:23–25).

Lament is necessary for individuals. We all experience suffering in our lives: sickness, poverty, abuse, alienation, drugs, violence, death. Things are not right. The first step to grief and healing is to move from overwhelmed silence to speech, the bold speech of lament. The Psalms show us how to speak out against suffering and oppression, even against God. But such crying out allows us both to grieve and to grow into a mature covenant partner with God and not merely a subservient one.

Scripture scholar Walter Wink suggests a haunting image: "We human beings are far too frail and tiny to bear all this pain. . . . What we need is a portable form of the Wailing Wall in Jerusalem, where we can unburden ourselves of this accumulated suffering. We need to experience it; it is part of reality . . . . We are to articulate these agonizing longings and let them pass through us to God" (*Engaging the Powers*, Fortress Press, 1992).

Lament is also necessary for life in society, raising questions of justice and power. Another Scripture scholar, Walter Brueggemann, writes strongly: "For the managers of the system—political, economic, religious, moral—there is always a hope that the troubled folks will not notice the dysfunction or that a tolerance of a certain degree of dysfunction can be accepted as normal and necessary, even if unpleasant. Lament occurs when the dysfunction reaches an unacceptable level, when the injustice is intolerable and change is insisted upon."

He adds that when lament is not allowed, justice questions gradually become ignored. When this happens, we miss the public systemic issues about which "biblical faith is relentlessly concerned."

Lament allows us to move from silence to speech, from meditation to active hope. It renews and deepens our relationship with God, even as it questions and challenges God. Lament confronts the evils in our religion and culture, proclaiming that these must not be.

Lent provides a perfect time for this lament. Perhaps the Psalms or Lamentations can help you recognize your own experience. Perhaps you can simply create your own expression. This Lent, what in your life calls forth lament?

9

Fasting for Justice and Life

"**I**s such the fast that I choose, a day to humble oneself? Is it to bow down the head like a bulrush, and to lie in sackcloth and ashes? Will you call this a fast, a day acceptable to the LORD? Is not this the fast that I choose: to loose the bonds of injustice, to undo the thongs of the yoke, to let the oppressed go free, and to break every yoke? Is it not to share your bread with the hungry, and bring the homeless poor into your house; . . . Then your light shall break forth like the dawn" (Isaiah 58:5–8).

A bold proclamation, isn't it? And especially appropriate for us when we begin our observance of Lent. It is also a very old challenge, spoken around 500 B.C.E. by the unknown prophet (or disciples of a prophet) known simply as Third Isaiah.

(The words of Third Isaiah, who lived in Jerusalem after the people returned from exile in 539, were added to the message of Isaiah of Jerusalem who preached between 740 and 700. Another unknown prophet, Second Isaiah, encouraged the people near the end of their exile, 587–539. Our present biblical Book of Isaiah contains the messages of all three prophets: chapters 1–39 from Isaiah of Jerusalem, chapters 40–55 from Second Isaiah, chapters 56–66 from Third Isaiah.)

Jesus seems to have taken this message very seriously, for Luke begins his description of Jesus' public ministry by referring to it (Luke 4:16–21). Matthew also highlights the theme at the end of Jesus' ministry, in the dramatic last judgment scene: "for I was hungry and you gave me food . . . a stranger and you welcomed me . . . sick and you took care of me" (Matthew 25:31–46).

In our time, church leaders have consistently emphasized the same ideas: care for the poor and justice for the oppressed. The Synod of Bishops in 1971 stated that working for justice is "a constitutive dimension of the preaching of the Gospel." Again and again Pope John Paul II has promoted "solidarity," the recognition that we all are bound together and so must work for the universal common good. Our own bishops, following the lead of Cardinal Joseph Bernardin, have challenged us to live according to the consistent ethic of life.

During Lent, will we take seriously the words of Third Isaiah, Jesus, and the magisterium? What kind of "fasting" will we do? It is at least a little curious that our observance of Lent begins with ashes and requires giving up food, when these Scripture passages call us to so much more. Will these externals symbolize internal conversion and lead us to concrete actions?

Surely, we cannot do everything, but we can do one thing. And the possibilities are almost endless. Visit elderly friends or family in a nursing home. Learn why the Church opposes the death penalty and then write to the governor. Join a parish group that is trying to confront racism. Spend more time with your children. Seek reconciliation. Continue to support those suffering from hurricanes and earthquakes, including urging business leaders to respond in humanitarian, even Gospel-inspired ways. Volunteer in a soup kitchen. Ask for help in breaking an addiction.

Not only during Lent but throughout the year, how will you help create a culture of justice, love, and life?

10

Passion Past and Present

Jesus did not speak "seven last words." Although a favorite Good Friday topic, Jesus' final words are very different in some of the Gospels. In Mark's Gospel, for example, there is only one "word" (sentence): "My God, my God, why have you forsaken me?" (15:34).

In our hearts and minds, we blend together the four different passion narratives. (For more details and some excellent Holy Week reading and prayer, see Raymond Brown's little book *A Crucified Christ in Holy Week*, Liturgical Press, 1992.) It is easy to forget that the Gospels are not literal accounts but faith proclamations of the Good News of Jesus. As our Church teaches, apostolic faith and preaching reshaped the memories and traditions of Jesus' words and deeds. The Gospels, then, present four portraits (not photographs) of Jesus.

This Holy Week, we hear two strikingly different portraits of Jesus' passion and death. On Palm Sunday of the Lord's Passion we hear Mark's portrayal of the passion. On Good Friday, as always, we hear John's. Their dramatic differences allow us to appreciate the depths of Jesus' identity and experience, along with the richness of meaning for our lives.

Mark's account begins on a gloomy note in the garden, and the darkness intensifies until Jesus' death. The major theme is abandonment. All of the disciples flee, leaving Jesus completely alone. Jesus' only words on the cross are the opening of Psalm 22: "My God, my God, why have you forsaken me?"

The cry ought not to be softened. Jesus expresses the agony of feeling forsaken as he faces a terrible death. The scene fits Mark's theological outlook developed throughout his Gospel: people can become true disciples only through the suffering symbolized by the cross.

John's passion story is very, very different. Even in the midst of suffering and dying, John's Jesus is in control. The major theme is sovereignty. His power is expressed both in the garden and in the trial. John describes Jesus on the cross as speaking to fulfill Scripture and deliberately handing over his spirit.

Four notes: First, the passion stories invite our participation. If we are honest, we recognize that different aspects of our personality and history fit a wide range of characters in this drama.

Second, as we hear the passion stories, especially John's, we need to be aware of the anti-Jewish feelings. Rooted in the early bitterness between church and synagogue, these anti-Jewish elements have produced deadly memories and actions. Pope John Paul powerfully proclaimed the need for contrition and healing.

Third, the passion continues. Again and again we hear about—and experience—tragic suffering. The floods in Mozambique, the embargo in Iraq, drugs in our cities, violence in our families, cancer, AIDS: the list of suffering goes on and on and on.

Fourth, the passion and death of Jesus are not the end of the story. God vindicates Jesus' faithfulness by raising him from the dead. We remember the passion and death as an Easter people.

This Holy Week, as you enter the passion stories of past and present, ask yourself: "How will I respond?"

11

Why Did Jesus Live and Die?

Because the life, death, and resurrection of Jesus make up the foundation of Christianity, the Christian community has long reflected on their significance for our lives. What was the purpose of Jesus' life?

Within the Christian tradition, there has been a variety of attempts to answer this question. One view, deeply rooted in Scripture and probably most frequently handed on in everyday religion, is the understanding of Jesus' life, which emphasizes redemption. This view returns to the creation story and sees in Adam and Eve's sin a fundamental alienation from God, a separation so profound that God must intervene to overcome it. The Incarnation, the Word becoming flesh, is considered as God's action to right this original wrong. Redemption, then, is basically understood as a "buying back."

Popular piety has often expressed redemption in terms of "opening the gates of heaven" and Jesus "making up" for our sinfulness. This focus has especially centered on Jesus' passion and death, at times seeming to imply that an angry God demanded the Son's suffering as a necessary placating act. The purpose of Jesus' life is directly linked to original sin and all human sinfulness. Jesus, particularly by his passion and death, buys us back. Without original sin, there would have been no need for the Incarnation.

There exists in the Christian tradition, however, another perspective on the purpose of Jesus' life. This view emphasizes the Incarnation; indeed, it holds that the whole purpose of creation is for the Incarnation. The purpose of Jesus' life is the fulfillment of the whole creative process.

Because this view may be unfamiliar, the following scene may help explain it. Pretend for a moment that we can get into God's mind before creation has begun. God thinks: "I want to share my love and life completely and definitively. But in order to do that there has to be something out there to receive it. I want to become human—but I must first create humanity!"

Incarnation, in this view, is not an afterthought, something necessary only as a result of original sin. Incarnation, God's sharing life and love, is the first thought, the original purpose for all of creation.

From this perspective, God is appreciated with a different emphasis. God is not an angry or vindictive God, demanding the suffering and death of Jesus as a payment for past sin. God is, instead, a gracious God, sharing divine life and love in creation and in the Incarnation.

So, why Jesus' life? Jesus is the whole purpose of creation. God loves us so greatly as to want to share divine life with us in an irrevocable way by becoming human. Jesus is the model of full human life; he calls us to live this life as his disciples.

Why Jesus' death? In faithfulness to his call, Jesus embodied and proclaimed the Reign of God. In doing so, he upset and alarmed the powers-that-be, who finally sentenced him to capital punishment.

This holy season, what does the life and death of Jesus mean for you?

12

Emmaus and the Moral Life

E aster season offers us a number of wonderful and meaningful scenes from the Gospels: Mary Magdalene as the first apostle of the Resurrection, doubting Thomas, Jesus preparing breakfast at the Sea of Galilee. My favorite is the story of the two disciples journeying from Jerusalem to Emmaus.

The two disciples, despairing over the tragic events of Good Friday, hear the news of the empty tomb but pay no attention. Instead they leave Jerusalem. A "stranger" joins them along the way, first listening to their broken hopes, then enlightening them by using their Scriptures. Still, they do not see clearly. Only after they have offered hospitality do they recognize the Risen Jesus in the breaking of the bread.

What an exquisite story! Surely it is the story not just of two disciples but of the early Christian community. Struggling to find meaning in the horrible death of Jesus, they must have searched their Scriptures (what is often now called the Old Testament) for insight. They met together to remember and tell stories of Jesus' teaching and healing. They broke bread together—and in this whole context, they encountered the Risen Jesus in their midst.

They saw clearly who Jesus was and what he meant for their lives. Their hearts were "burning within" as they listened. They found new hope and energy, and so went out to others to proclaim the Good News.

Their story is our story. But is it really? Do our hearts burn with excitement when we hear God's word proclaimed. Does the breaking of the bread give us new hope and energy? Or is our liturgy mostly boring routine, merely a weekly obligation?

And what does Emmaus have to do with the moral life? Everything! Christian morality is primarily not about following laws but about accepting and responding to God's gracious love and call. We embody our response in all the details of how we live life (here's where laws provide helpful guidance): loving others, being faithful to commitments, working for justice. Our relationship with God is the very heart of morality.

The celebration of the Eucharist—our Emmaus today—is clearly an essential part of developing this relationship. As those first two disciples did, so too we bring our broken hopes and despairing hearts—questions of personal suffering, youthful violence and murder, ethnic cleansing, oppression of all kinds—to be enlightened and encouraged by the Scriptures. We bring both our joy and trust and our blindness and hardness of heart to encounter the Risen Jesus in our breaking bread together.

If we do find and help create nourishing liturgies and communities, then our relationship with God will take on new life and importance. We will find energy and hope and vision to reach out to others, to confront the evil powers in economic and religious and political structures, to resist the competing messages about the meaning of life that we receive from TV and advertising. In short, if we experience Emmaus, we will live as faithful disciples.

What do you need to live a moral life?

13

Light in the Darkness

During the past few years we seem to have experienced more darkness and death than light and life. Ethnic cleansing, refugee suffering, terrorist attacks, massive bombing—all are horrors that most of us cannot begin to comprehend. We do experience, however, and grieve over debilitating disease, unexpected death, and suicides among our families and friends. Tornado destruction and death also shock and stun our community. The shootings and violence at the school in Colorado and the destruction of the World Trade Center buildings overwhelm us. Darkness and death—too much darkness and death—threaten to silence our Easter Alleluias and to smother our joy and hope.

What can we do? What ought we to do? Surely, we must begin simply by acknowledging the extensive and intense suffering. We must not hide from or deny this harsh reality. In *Engaging the Powers*, Scripture scholar Walter Wink speaks directly to this point: "We human beings are far too frail and tiny to bear all this pain. . . . What we need is a portable form of the Wailing Wall in Jerusalem, where we can unburden ourselves of this accumulated suffering. . . . We are to articulate these agonizing longings and let them pass through us to God."

So, we acknowledge the pain and pray. We must also act. "Social action without prayer is soulless; but prayer without action lacks integrity." Wink adds his prayer: "God, help me to refuse ever to accept evil; by your Spirit empower me to work for change precisely where and how you call me; and free me from thinking I have to do everything."

If each of us must prayerfully discern his or her own specific call to action, we can at least begin together by naming the evil. Was there evil at Columbine High School? More than enough: mockery and alienation, bombs and guns, sick cyberspace and Nazi symbols, hatred and suffering and death.

Already the discussion, however, is slipping into political stereotypes. One side emphasizes values and the media; the other, gun control. Surely, the situation in Littleton includes both personal and social, behavioral and structural. All facets of life deserve—and need—attention.

Was there evil in Kosovo and Serbia? More than enough: ethnic cleansing, the suffering of refugees, NATO bombing, hatred and death. Is the bombing justified? How can we ordinary citizens even judge, when complete and accurate information is so hard to find?

Was there evil in the hijacked planes the terrorists turned into human missiles? Again, much more than enough. Was the continuous retaliation bombing truly the "last resort"? Did we miss opportunities to think and act in creative nonviolent ways? Should we really be surprised when some of our children turn to guns and bombs to resolve conflicts when our government does the very same thing?

Columbine and Kosovo and the destruction of the World Trade Center stand as tragic symbols in our culture of violence and death and of our urgent need for a profound renewal and transformation. This healing must reach to the depths of our personal and communal lives. A sound basis for this renewal certainly is the consistent ethic of life, leading us to proclaim the story of Jesus again and again, to care for each other gently and persistently, and to engage faithfully the powers that dehumanize us all.

We begin each Easter season in the darkness of the vigil service, waiting for the spark of new light. In the darkness of our world now, how will you be a little light?

14

Ancient Cities, Living Stones

"Come to [the Lord], a living stone, though rejected by mortals yet chosen and precious in God's sight, and like living stones, let yourselves be built into a spiritual house . . ." (1 Peter 2:4–5).

This passage from the First Letter of Peter, along with the rest of chapters one and two, invites us to ponder the rich meaning of our baptism. It helps us to appreciate both the dignity of our calling and the challenges of living in holiness—even in the midst of suffering and persecution.

The passage also helps me to process a remarkable journey. Catholic Theological Union in Chicago sponsored a study tour to ancient and early-Christian sites in Syria and Jordan, with short trips into Turkey and Lebanon included. We visited Antioch and Damascus, Ebla and Apamea, several more cities of the Decapolis, and numerous other places. The travel was enriching and wearying.

We saw, of course, the many stones of ancient cities. Often these ruins were very impressive. As the First Letter of Peter reminds us, however, the living stones are of greatest importance. Here are two examples from our travels.

In a remote part of northwestern Syria stand the ruins of a once-magnificent church—indeed, when it was built in honor of Simon Stylites in the fifth century, it was the largest in the world. After Christianity had become the religion of the Roman Empire and the threat of martyrdom ceased, some people sought out lives of heroic asceticism. Some moved to the desert; others sat on the top of large pillars. That is where Simon spent thirty-eight years of his life!

Surely, few of us can understand or appreciate this form of piety. Yet, in the fifth century, it captured people's imaginations and hearts. Simon became a wisdom figure; people came for counseling and direction. And when he died they build a grand church on the top of a windswept hill.

Hundreds of feet in front of the entrance stands a separate chapel, which is really just the baptistry, the place of baptism. What an awe-filled ritual baptism must have been for these people: to step down into the font, to come up into new life, and then to make the long procession into the church. Old stones helped us to recall the faith of "living stones," the same faith we profess fifteen hundred years later.

Across the border in Turkey is the city of Antioch (called Antakya today). Antioch, of course, was a major city for early Christianity, where Jesus' followers were first called Christians. Perhaps two of our Gospels come from this area.

Today, however, there are few old stones in the modern city, only a grotto church commemorating Peter's presence in Antioch. But there are living stones. We visited the small Roman Catholic Church and spoke with the pastor and members of the community (which has about fifty people). They work closely with the larger Orthodox community and are in dialogue with the much larger Muslim community. More powerfully than the grotto, these living stones expressed not only our long history but also the dignity and challenges of our shared faith.

Travel to different cultures and ancient cities can inspire renewing perspectives. But a prayerful reading of Scripture can do the same. First Peter reminds us that once we were "not a people" but now we are "God's people." What does your baptism mean for your everyday life?

15

A New Month for Choosing Life

I n an October editorial, the *Catholic Telegraph* got it exactly right when it stated that one month is not enough for demonstrating our commitment to life. The month of October is set aside as "Respect Life Month," with particular emphasis on the first Sunday. It is, of course, helpful to have these special celebrations. They remind us of God's blessings and challenge us to raise our awareness and renew our commitment.

Choosing life, however, must be a year-round activity. As we turn the calendar page from October to November, our valuing of life ought not to lose any of its focus or energy.

The first days of the new month offer opportunities to reflect on and to live the Gospel of Life. Our remembrances of all saints and all souls direct our attention to God's wonderful gifts of life and faith. We celebrate life, and with trust in our gracious and faithful God we look ahead to the fullness of new life. These feast days can also lead us both to pray about our own dying and death and to take some concrete action.

What action? Filling out an "advance directive"—a living will or durable power of attorney for health care. These forms allow us to state the kind of treatment we desire if we reach a point when we are no longer able to make this decision. The Catholic tradition has long taught that only ethically ordinary means of life support must be used. Our tradition has also emphasized that life is a basic good but not an absolute one. We would not, for example, break our relationship with God in order to save our life. The saints, especially the martyrs, are dramatic witnesses of this truth. So, the tradition holds, we do not have to do "everything possible" to keep a person alive. An advance directive (your doctor, lawyer, or local hospital can provide a form for you) can help you be clear with your family and physician about your wishes concerning these matters.

Another event early in November—elections—raises the question of our commitment to life. The Church, especially the teachings of the U.S. bishops, has long provided guidance in this complex area. The consistent ethic of life has become a key part of the bishops' moral teaching. Pope John Paul II affirmed similar themes in his 1995 encyclical *The Gospel of Life*.

The consistent ethic of life challenges our usual political affiliations. It calls us to evaluate candidates and public policy in light of the Gospel, not party platforms. It is worth repeating the bishops' statement from *Political Responsibility:* "Our moral framework does not easily fit the categories of right or left, Republican or Democrat. We are called to measure every party and movement by how its agenda touches human life and human dignity."

If we are to be consistent, we must direct our attention to abortion and euthanasia but also to welfare and immigration, sexism and racism, capital punishment and health-care reform, trade agreements and sweatshops, education and the environment. Taking seriously the consistent ethic of life transforms voting into a complex and challenging responsibility.

What steps will you take each new month to choose life?

~ 16 ~

The Cost of Discipleship

M id-November brings a very special but sad anniversary. On November 16, 1989, in the middle of the night, members of the El Salvador military murdered six Jesuits along with their housekeeper and her daughter. In their work at the University of Central America, the Jesuits preached the Gospel and attempted to apply the social teachings of the Church to the Salvadoran reality of poverty and oppression. For this they were threatened and called Communists. For this they had their brains blown out—literally—by powerful weapons.

(Among the killers were men trained by American servicemen on American soil. If you hear of protests to close the School of the Americas—or whatever our government now calls it—this deadly event is one of the reasons.)

November also brings the end of the liturgical year. In the Gospel we follow Jesus on the way to Jerusalem, and he instructs his disciples—and now us—about the meaning and cost of discipleship. Jesus also teaches about a suffering messiah.

It may be helpful to remember that in Jesus' time there was an expectation of a messiah. But this messiah was to be successful, a powerful winner. Jesus was not. His first followers had to deal with the fact of his terrible death. So they searched their Scriptures to find light to help interpret their experience.

In the Psalms, in the Suffering Servant passages, and in other texts they did find help, which colored and shaped their stories. Not all interpretation, however, and certainly not all pieties have faithfully reflected the God revealed by Jesus. This God is a God of life and love, of compassion and justice and nonviolence. In no way could this God demand the suffering, torture, and death of Jesus. The Powers did that—and still do. Faithful disciples face the cross in the dramatic and in the ordinary. The God of Jesus surely does not desire this, but instead leads us as individuals and as community in resisting evil.

For the UCA Jesuits and the two women (and so many others), the cost of discipleship was indeed dramatic. For most of us the cost comes in everyday ways:

- the tension in our hearts and families generated by living in a consumer society flooded with advertising,
- the temptation promoted by media to solve difficult situations with violence,
- the sadness of confronting oppressive systems in society and religion,
- the challenge of feeding the hungry in a world that ignores the common good,
- the pain of encountering the dark mystery of illness of all kinds.

What to do? Jesus has certainly offered us the way:

- radical trust in a compassionate and present God,
- forgiveness,
- bold actions that break down barriers and old alienations,
- solidarity and tender love,
- and, yes, the willingness to accept the implications of faithfulness to God's call.

What is the cost of discipleship in your life these days?

~ 17 ~

For the New Year: Truth and Life

For many of us, New Year's resolutions come and go. Perhaps these two will come and stay: seek the truth and choose life.

In the days and weeks just before the new year of 1999, our nation simultaneously experienced two striking events: the renewed bombing of Iraq and the impeachment of President Clinton. These dramatic events undoubtedly overshadowed other stories, such as the possibility of the Senate ending the ban on embryo research, the success of abortion-rights groups in state courts, the likelihood of Ohio executing a prisoner who may be mentally ill.

At the very center of all these stories are truth and life.

Long ago, Pontius Pilate asked, "What is truth?" It is a question that our country needs to consider carefully—and, of course, we as individuals too! Take, for example, the impeachment process. Isn't it amazing that only a handful of members of the House of Representatives crossed "party lines" on the two articles that were approved? How could the search for truth among 434 people end in such a split? Was the search too heavily influenced by party affiliation?

As we struggle with moral dilemmas and what we ought to do, we too experience particular pressures and influences: from our wealth and class, from our business or union connections, from our deep desires and family histories. All of these influences color, and perhaps even distort, our search for the truth. Good intentions alone do not make moral decisions (nor do focus groups or public opinion polls). The desire to stop a patient's suffering, for example, does not justify killing the patient. Similarly, naming the deed an "act of mercy" does not make it one.

No, truth is beyond an individual's private desires and determination. The Catholic tradition holds that reality is the basis of morality. Reality is God, human beings, and the rest of creation—all in relationship. Every moral dilemma presents a small but real slice of this totality.

As Cardinal Joseph Bernardin wrote, there is an "objective, albeit imperfectly perceived, moral order." Our task is to use wisdom sources (Scripture, church teaching, experience, etc.) to help us perceive the reality as accurately as we are able, including its conflicting values and obligations. And then act so that life may truly flourish.

Life is the heart of reality. Cardinal Bernardin, as we have seen, spoke eloquently about the consistent ethic of life. This moral framework cuts across "party lines" to affirm the value and dignity of life from womb to tomb. From abortion and research on embryos to capital punishment and the bombing of Iraq, the life ethic challenges individuals and governments to choose life consistently—personally, nationally, globally.

Choosing life does not imply passivity in the face of evil. Rather, as Walter Wink has expressed it, the question is: "How can we oppose evil without creating new evils and being made evil ourselves?" His book, *Engaging the Powers*, offers a detailed, scripturally-rooted description of creative and active nonviolence—and lists many examples of its success!

For any new year, what will it mean for you to seek the truth and to choose life?

～ 18 ～

Remembering the Great Jubilee

Where were you for the coming of the new millennium? Some people were anticipating some kind of disaster, so they stocked up food and other supplies in their homes. Some were even preparing something like a bomb shelter. TV shows and movies dramatized citizens barricading their property.

Advertisements also suggested where people would be—exotic places like the Great Wall in China or the pyramids in Egypt. Other folks were planning a whirlwind tour around the world. (It is not surprising that we commercialized this special time.)

A third option had nothing to do with a spot on the globe—any place would do just fine—but with where you were in understanding and celebrating the true spirit of this rare event. What did the two thousandth anniversary of Jesus' birth mean for you? Do the biblical themes of the Great Jubilee still influence your life—your relationship with God, with other people, with our world?

The roots of Jubilee are found in the Bible. Because the Hebrews experienced the pain of Egypt's oppression, when the Israelite tribes gained control of the land of Canaan, they desired to set up a different political and economic structure, one free of oppression. They stressed community and the fair distribution of land. The tribes developed laws to protect these basic values related to their family structure and their farming economy.

The Book of Leviticus gives the most significant instruction (see 25:10–12). Those who had lost their land because of debts would get the land back. Those who had been sold into slavery would be freed to return to their families. And all would be reminded how God freed and chose them as God's people. All would be reminded how all of creation, especially the land, belonged to God and was God's gift.

Jubilee themes are found in Jesus' life, beginning with his keynote address in Nazareth (see Luke 4:14–30). Jesus, the Anointed One, teaches and heals and proclaims the presence of God's Reign. Jesus is the fulfillment of God's promises for the hungry, the sick, the imprisoned. Truly, it is the year of the Lord's favor!

Jesus' keynote address leads us to refocus our attention on who we are and what we do by contemplating the identity and mission of Jesus. With Jesus, we are called and anointed. With Jesus, we are sent out to teach, to heal, to free. With Jesus, we face conflict and rejection. With Jesus, we reach out to all with compassion, especially the economically, physically, and socially poor. With Jesus, we proclaim with passion glad tidings of healing and hope.

Our U.S. bishops invited us to apply this vision and commitment to our everyday lives by taking and living the "Jubilee Pledge." Themes of prayer and service are just as urgent today.

Where were you for the new millennium: trapped in Y2K fears, caught up in elaborate parties, or inspired by Jubilee themes of charity, justice, and peace? Where are you today?

PART III

Meaning, Morality, and Society

*In no other age has humanity enjoyed such an
abundance of wealth, resources and economic well-being;
and yet a huge proportion of the people of the world
is plagued by hunger and extreme need while countless
numbers are totally illiterate. At no time have people had
such a keen sense of freedom, only to be faced by new
forms of social and psychological slavery. The world
is keenly aware of its unity and of mutual
interdependence in essential solidarity,
but at the same time it is split into bitterly opposing
camps. We have not yet seen the last of bitter political,
social, and economic hostility, and racial and ideological
antagonism, nor are we free from the
spectre of a war of total destruction.*

Pastoral Constitution on the Church in the Modern World, 4

19

The Questioning of Meaning and Morality

I s raising questions about our beliefs and morals a threat to our relationship with God or to life in the Church? Vatican II did not think so! Instead, following Pope John XXIII's lead, the council saw new questions as an opportunity for "a more accurate and penetrating grasp of the faith. . . . For the deposit of faith or revealed truths are one thing; the manner in which they are formulated without violence to their meaning and significance is another" (*Pastoral Constitution on the Church in the Modern World*, 62).

Human beings necessarily live in and are influenced by a particular time and place and culture; no one can stand outside of history. Every human expression is limited to particular concepts and perspectives. "Limited," of course, does not mean untrue, but is a reminder that no one possesses complete objectivity and all understanding.

In the same way, church teachings and even Scripture are limited. It simply cannot be otherwise. We can discover truth, but along the way we may find clearer ways to express it. That is what Vatican II is affirming.

In their introduction to Karl Rahner's *The Practice of Faith* (Crossroad/Herder & Herder, 1984), Bishop Karl Lehmann and Albert Raffelt have expressed a similar insight: "God's response never fails to transcend our capacity to ask questions, and the spiritually alert Christian, indeed the human being as human being, must continue to swing the hard, sober hammer of inquiry. There are no forbidden questions, then, nor any false pride in some inviolable, final 'possession' of understanding."

Simply stated, we must always ask questions. We must not grow complacent with given answers. We must search to see truth more clearly. All this means hard work!

Why is this insight so important? Because we are tempted to stop too soon in our search for the truth about meaning and morality in our lives. We are tempted merely to accept past answers and explanations, even when there are valid reasons for questioning these answers. In fact, many of us were raised to respond with this almost blind obedience; some in the Church today would still have us act this way.

Such a response, however, as indicated in the quotations above, would undermine who we are as Christians and as human beings. We would short-circuit the search for truth.

Let me give you an example. My chapter on homosexuality and church teaching (see chapter 36) includes some questions about the tradition's understanding of homosexual actions. These questions are rooted in contemporary understanding of Scripture, in the recognition of deep-seated prejudice, and in careful attention to people's experience. Questions do not necessarily lead to change. But we must ask the questions, so that the Church does not get stuck in incomplete or even wrong teaching. In our tradition's history, happily, people did ask questions about the Church's positions on slavery, on economics, on the death penalty. In these areas, questions did lead to change, to a "more accurate and penetrating grasp" of truth.

Swinging "the hard, sober hammer of inquiry" requires openness yet faithfulness, recognition of the possibility of mistakes yet the willingness to risk. Will you risk the hard work of asking questions in a spirit of committed faithfulness?

~ 20 ~

Tensions in the Church—
Past and Present

Shortly before his death, Cardinal Joseph Bernardin announced the Catholic Common Ground Initiative, an effort to overcome divisiveness in the Church. He stated, "The unity of the Church is threatened, the great gift of the Second Vatican Council is in danger of being seriously undermined, the faithful members of the Church are weary, and our witness to government, society and culture is compromised."

The purpose of the project was to bring people together for dialogue leading to mutual understanding. Reactions to the project from most of the other cardinals and from liberal and conservative groups only seemed to underline the separation, fear, and suspicion within the Church.

Many experiences in various dioceses indicate that we still live in a very nervous Church. Two in particular—the renovation of churches and new ministry for gays and lesbians—have evoked a wide range of responses. Some have expressed hurt or anger, some even bitterness and meanspiritedness. These latter ones seem especially far removed from the Gospel.

Sadly, such division and suspicion and even prejudice are not new in the Church. Two examples from early Christianity will serve as sober reminders of this fact. The Council of Ephesus met in 431 to discuss the Church's teaching about Jesus' identity. This was a time of serious debates (much more than can be discussed here) between bishops. At Ephesus, Cyril of Alexandria, acting on a commission given him by the pope, opened the council—even though many bishops, particularly the supporters of his opponent Nestorius, had not yet arrived. Cyril's council condemned Nestorius. When the other bishops arrived, they held a separate council which excommunicated Cyril! It took several years to work out an agreement.

A second example is John Chrysostom, a doctor of the Church. After being ordained in 386, John spent twelve years in Antioch as preacher, Scripture scholar, and moralist. Then he was selected to be Patriarch of Constantinople. His energetic reforms and bold preaching angered many, including the Patriarch of Alexandria, leading to political and church intrigue and even to attempts on John's life. Finally, the emperor forced John into exile (where he died in 407).

If there is a curious consolation in the horrors of history (at least bishops in our country do not have to worry about exile), the Church today cannot accept our real—if less dramatic—suspicions and divisions. These simply contradict the Gospel, keeping us from loving one another and from creating a culture of life.

The spirit of the Common Ground Initiative points us in the right direction. For some additional thoughts on the tensions in our Church, I encourage you to research and read "Divisions, Dialogue and the Catholicity of the Church" by Thomas Rausch, S.J., in *America*, January 31, 1998. You may want to read prayerfully the letter to the Ephesians, especially chapter four. And then ask yourself how your words and actions are helping to build up the Body of Christ.

21

Suffering

S uffering surrounds us. Genocide and wars cause death beyond comprehension. Violence in many forms rips our cities apart, yet continues to be glorified on TV and in movies. Abuse victimizes innocent people, almost destroying the human spirit. The list could go on and on and on. Undoubtedly, you can add your own examples from your life and the lives of family and friends.

Suffering surrounds us—and has always confronted the human family. For thousands of years people have been searching for some meaning in suffering, have been asking "Why?" In the Bible, Job wrestled with suffering and with God. The early Christian community struggled to make sense of the horrible torture and execution of Jesus. Theologians have tried to hold suffering together with God's power, justice, love—and human freedom.

Yet, for all the struggle and searching, no simple answer has been found. Some attempts at responding to suffering are profoundly troublesome, even some found in our Catholic tradition. Through the ages, suffering has been explained as God's will or as God testing us or punishing us. At times God has even been described as demanding Jesus' suffering and death as a means of atonement—to appease an angry God.

What a distorted image of God! What a terrible contradiction of the God revealed by Jesus! No good parent would desire the torture and death of his or her child. The God Jesus describes in his parables is a forgiving and loving God. Think of the parable of the prodigal son, for example.

So, what can be said about suffering? Surely we must first acknowledge the pain and horror of suffering, and we must never glorify it. Yes, suffering can lead us to deeper maturity and wisdom. But suffering can also crush the human spirit. We must never seek suffering, but, following the life and ministry of Jesus, always work as individuals and as community to overcome and end suffering. Still, as with Jesus' own life, we recognize that fidelity to our life of discipleship—embodying a consistent ethic of life in personal, political, and economic choices—may be costly, may lead to suffering. The many martyrs of our own time are dramatic examples, but this cost faces all of us in many ordinary ways too.

We acknowledge the horror of suffering, suffering which results from others' evil choices and that which simply happens (for example, from a tornado). And finally, with Job and searchers throughout history, we stand before suffering's incomprehensibility and God's remarkable respect of human freedom. Suffering remains a profound mystery.

Even though the human response to suffering usually includes the "Why?" question, it may be more helpful to ask: "How can I respond? What can we do now?" Some suggestions: (1) trusting in a gracious God of life (who may seem very distant); (2) remembering and telling in our church the story of the life and death and resurrection of Jesus; (3) embodying God's love by remaining with others in their suffering; (4) searching in solidarity with others for creative and courageous ways to overcome suffering and its causes in our world.

How are you suffering? What is your response?

22

God and Suffering

In the last chapter, I reflected with you on the incomprehensibility of suffering. Throughout the centuries, human beings have searched for meaning in suffering, especially the suffering of innocent people. We still ask "Why?" But we have not discovered a convincing answer. Rather, we seem to be led by life to acknowledge that we cannot neatly explain suffering, but instead must find ways to respond in trust and in solidarity with others to this troubling experience.

Theologians have long wrestled with the mystery of God and the mystery of suffering. How can God's omnipotence and love and justice and the reality of suffering be held together? Can God suffer with us? Does this mean that God changes in some way?

The Scriptures can help us find appropriate ways to speak of God. We hear of a God who creates, who is very involved in people's lives leading them to liberation, who forms a covenant, who becomes one of us, who heals and enlightens, who brings Jesus to new life after death.

Surely this God cares for us and loves us. Surely, in some way, this God must suffer with us in our suffering. How could it be otherwise for the loving creator, the covenantal partner, the tender and gracious parent?

Indeed, we must be careful in our God-talk. We must not try to create God in our image. We must respect the otherness, the transcendence, the incomprehensibility of God—who is Holy Mystery.

We must also be careful not even to imply that God wants or demands suffering—either ours or Jesus'.

I suggest the following image for your meditation. Recall Michelangelo's magnificent sculpture *Pieta*. The grieving mother of Jesus holds his dead body in her arms. Feel the pain, the sorrow, the horror. Then allow the sculpture to become a symbol, to take on even greater meanings. First, perhaps, the symbol of the world's mothers holding their battered sons and daughters, victims of wars and other violence. Then let the sculpture speak of a gentle God holding God's torn and bloodied world. Finally, let it be God holding your broken spirit.

Our God suffers with us. In the depths of suffering we too may cry out: "My God, my God, why have you forsaken me?" In the darkness, we may need to express our lament, even defiance, but finally our trust that the gracious, gentle God holds our broken bodies and spirits.

We can trust because there is more: our God is a God of resurrection, of new life. The story did not end with the cross, with suffering and death. No, God raised Jesus to new and transformed life. And we are an Easter people. This truth, ultimately, is at the very heart of our response to suffering. God suffers with us, leads us as individuals and as community in resisting evil, and brings us all to the fullness of life.

What does this Good News mean for you today?

23

Politics and Ethics

For many of us, the time when elections end probably means a great relief: no more name calling, slanted statistics, attack advertising. Still, even though we may be tempted to be cynical, we also recognize just how important elections are.

So do the American bishops. For recent presidential election years, the Administrative Board of the United States Catholic Conference issued the statement I referred to in chapter 1 called *Political Responsibility*. The 1996 subtitle indicates the fundamental concerns of the bishops: *Proclaiming the Gospel of Life, Protecting the Least Among Us, and Pursuing the Common Good.* Embedded in the political issues are profound religious and ethical questions.

With this document, the bishops seek to provide guidance concerning these questions. They emphasize: "We are called to measure every party and movement by how its agenda touches human life and human dignity. For example, we stand with various religious and other groups to protect the unborn and defend the family; we also insist that a test of public advocacy is how public policies touch the poor and the weak. A key question is where are 'the least among us' in any national agenda?" (p. 6).

Political Responsibility summarizes the bishops' positions regarding twenty major topics, all rooted in the moral framework of the consistent ethic of life. To give a sense of the guidance, here are a few excerpts. On capital punishment: "The Church's commitment to the value and dignity of human life leads us to oppose the use of the death penalty. We believe that a return to the use of the death penalty is further eroding respect for life in our society" (p. 16). On discrimination and racism: "Signs of increased racial hostility poison our society. . . . It must be aggressively resisted by every individual and rooted out of every social institution and structure" (p. 17). On the economy: "The economy must be at the service of all people, especially the poor" (p. 18). On euthanasia: "We reject any law or social policy that sanctions suicide or assisted suicide or any deliberate and direct hastening of death for seriously ill patients" (p. 20). On welfare reform: "The goal of reform is reducing poverty and dependency, not cutting resources and programs" (p. 30).

What is our challenge as faithful disciples and as involved citizens? Where do we even begin? First, we can examine our conscience and prayerfully reflect on our reactions to politics. Has cynicism crept into our life? Second, we need to seek out information by reading carefully *Political Responsibility* and other appropriate material. Then we need to discuss the issues with families and friends and parish and community members. Does the Gospel or a particular political party shape our fundamental values and commitments? Third, we must vote. This may not be as simple as it seems. The choices are usually not very clear, for the platforms and policies of the political parties do not embody the consistent ethic of life.

The issues are urgent; our challenges are great. At each election, how will you choose life?

24

Super Tuesday and the Gospel

The opportunity to vote in a presidential primary raises a vital question: What really forms the basis of our political choices? Perhaps it is our longstanding commitment to a particular political party. Perhaps it is our race or gender or economic class. Perhaps it is simply the most convincing TV commercial. Perhaps it is the Gospel.

The Gospel? Indeed, for as disciples of Jesus, we want the Good News to be the very center of our lives, enlightening all our choices. Sober realism leads us to acknowledge, however, that some of the other influences often carry more weight.

The overlapping of the primaries and the season of Lent may just be a marvelous coincidence, then, a time for a change of heart, a time to take seriously our Gospel commitment when we make political choices. Help is available for all of us who want to take this process seriously.

As they had done through their administrative board for the previous six presidential elections, the U.S. bishops issued a statement on political responsibility for the 2000 elections. It is a revised and briefer document. "Faithful Citizenship: Civic Responsibility for a New Millennium" highlights some key challenges of our country, poses ten questions about human dignity and the common good, discusses the relationship between faith and politics, summarizes major themes of Catholic social teaching, and addresses four areas of national and global concern.

"Faithful Citizenship" deserves careful reading, prayerful reflection, serious discussion and action—a perfect Lenten practice. The statement also includes a long list of earlier documents from the NCCB/USCC, encouraging even more in-depth study of public policy issues.

Here, a brief look at a few details in the bishops' statement can serve both as an invitation to more careful study and as a sampler before primary voting. Among the challenges the bishops cite are the hate and intolerance infecting our society, the powerful economy which widens the gaps between rich and poor, the violence of ethnic cleansing and religious persecution.

One of their questions follows the lead of Pope John Paul II and his deep concern about a culture of death. Why does our nation turn to violence—to abortion, the death penalty, euthanasia—to solve difficult problems?

"Faithful Citizenship" reaffirms the bishops' conviction that a consistent ethic of life is the moral framework from which to address all political, economic, and social issues. The document collects these issues under four categories: protecting human life, promoting family life, pursuing social justice, practicing global solidarity.

The bishops acknowledge the difficulty of being faithful citizens and it is worth saying again: "Our moral framework does not easily fit the categories of right or left, Democrat or Republican." Still, they hope for a renewed political vitality, rooted in the values of the Gospel and church teaching.

"Faithful Citizenship" addresses the fundamental question of what it means to be a believer and a citizen. How will you respond this year and in years to come?

25

Profits and a Prophet's Death

A prophet died in 1999. Archbishop Helder Câmara, widely known as a defender of the poor, was ninety when he went home to the God he loved and served so well. Archbishop Câmara had been bishop of Olinda and Recife, a very poor area of Brazil.

His love of the Scriptures and his experiences with the people led Archbishop Câmara to become a strong advocate of social justice. He promoted land redistribution and better access to education. He criticized economic policies that valued profits more than people. He helped the church of South America to take seriously its responsibility to live in solidarity with the poor.

Not surprisingly, Archbishop Câmara's words and actions led to opposition, criticism, even death threats. His often-noted quotation gives us a sense of this twentieth-century prophet: "When I fed the poor, they called me a saint. When I asked, 'Why are they poor?' they called me a Communist."

His comment still challenges us today. Do we dare ask: Why are they poor? Are Gospel commitments at the heart of our response—or only economic systems and political theories?

Wrestling with ethical dilemmas is rarely an easy task. Confronting the ethical questions embedded in economics and politics is especially difficult. Often the issues are so very complex. Sometimes the realities are hidden from us—where are Olinda and Recife and what is life like there? Sometimes we may not see (or may not want to see) the poor in our midst. Sometimes, perhaps, we do respond—but with values rooted primarily in a profit-centered economy or in a particular political party. What is missing is the vision of the prophets and Jesus.

Here are a few issues from recent headlines. Admittedly, each is complicated. Each also embodies a profound ethical dilemma: the decisions and actions either promote or undermine the human flourishing of thousands, even millions, of our sisters and brothers.

- Welfare reform: Some studies show that more poor people are working but are worse off because of the recent reforms.
- Sanctions against Iraq: Reports point to the sanctions' deadly impact on children and the sick and elderly in Iraq.
- Debt relief for very poor countries: Many people and groups (including Pope John Paul II) called for the forgiveness of debts as a way to celebrate Jubilee 2000.

What can one person do? Get informed and get involved! Surely we cannot do everything, but we can do something—even in the midst of our many other responsibilities. I repeat: Take time to read the U.S. bishops' letter *Economic Justice for All*, their recent brief statement "A Catholic Framework for Economic Life," or their reports on the above issues. Contact Bread for the World to learn how you and your parish can be part of the efforts to help end hunger. Sift through political rhetoric and vote wisely—and do not hesitate to contact politicians at all levels.

As a faithful disciple of Jesus (see Matthew 25:31–46), Archbishop Câmara was willing to confront economic and political issues. How will you?

∼ **26** ∼

Engaging the Powers of Culture

Frequently in this book I mention the consistent ethic of life. Rooted in the life and teachings of Jesus, this moral vision has become a centerpiece of the teachings of the American Catholic bishops. The consistent ethic of life links together many different issues, cuts across liberal and conservative viewpoints, and challenges us to respect all life (for example, the life in the womb, the life of a criminal, the life on welfare, the life of the dying).

Now I would like to encourage you to read two books that I have used in my university classes. Neither uses the phrase "consistent ethic of life," but both help us to appreciate its meaning and challenge. The two books are the aforementioned *Engaging the Powers* by Walter Wink (Fortress Press, 1992) and the revised edition of *Following Christ in a Consumer Society* by John F. Kavanaugh (Orbis Books, 1991)—this revised edition has a bright yellow cover with "(Still)" inserted before the title.

Walter Wink is a Scripture scholar who has written extensively on the "principalities and powers" (see Colossians 1:15–20, for example). Wink gives us an appropriate contemporary understanding of these biblical images. "Every Power tends to have a visible pole, an outer form—be it a church, a nation, or an economy—and an invisible pole, an inner spirit or driving force that animates, legitimates, and regulates its physical manifestation in the world." Wink helps us to realize that every organized system has an inner spirituality. If this system has become oppressive, then "any attempt to transform a social system without addressing both its spirituality and its outer forms is doomed to failure."

Engaging the Powers begins with this haunting question: "How can we oppose evil without creating new evils and being made evil ourselves?" Wink goes on to describe the Powers at work in our culture, focusing especially on violence—violence in popular culture (including cartoons and movies), in nationalism, in foreign policy. Appealing to the example of Jesus, Wink describes an assertive nonviolence as the proper response to this evil system. He urges us to see oppressive parts of our lives (in church, nation, personal choices) that we really do not want to acknowledge. (A digest of Wink's writings, especially *Engaging the Powers*, has been published by Doubleday: *The Powers That Be,* 1998.)

John Kavanaugh in *(Still) Following Christ in a Consumer Society* also challenges us to live a consistent ethic of life. Kavanaugh focuses on other dimensions of our culture: materialism and consumerism. We turn things into people and people into things. In our society, more possessions mean more happiness.

Kavanaugh grounds his response in the life and teachings of Jesus. He describes how faithfully living the Christian life contradicts the values of a consumer society. Indeed, Kavanaugh writes, "Christianity at rock bottom radically conflicts with American culture, even subverts it."

Wink and Kavanaugh invite us to reconsider our values and priorities, to look again at the implications of the Scriptures for our everyday lives. Will you take the time and energy to read prayerfully (and discuss with others) these two books and risk hearing God's call in the context of our American culture?

27

In Guns We Trust

Violence saves. This ancient belief, never far from center stage of human actions, once again dramatically expressed itself in our society. How? Gun sales. In the final weeks of 1999 gun and ammunition sales surged; the FBI reported more than one million background checks just for handguns.

Why the huge increase in gun sales in 1999? Probably because of Y2K fears. Despite statements from police officials that bringing a gun into one's home is much more likely to cause harm than any possible Y2K rioting or lawlessness, people turned to guns to protect and save.

America's love affair with guns has often been documented. The belief that violence saves, however, is much, much older—older than the Bible itself. The ancient Babylonian creation story (the *Enuma Elish*) describes a rebellion among the gods. To protect one group and to create order, a younger god, Marduk, kills the mother god, Tiamat, and then stretches out her corpse to create the cosmos. Human origins are divine, but come from the blood of an assassinated god.

As Scripture scholar Walter Wink has pointed out, the heart of this story—that our origin is violence, that war brings peace—remains the central belief, the dominant religion, of our modern world. Throughout our lives, from cartoons and movies and TV to public policy, we are taught that might makes right. Violence works; it is inevitable.

Our religions both contradict and reinforce the belief in violence. The first creation story in the Bible is diametrically opposed to the Babylonian view. In Genesis, a good God creates a good world. Good is prior to evil; violence has no part in creation. However, belief in violence, though often challenged by the prophets, gradually infected Jewish convictions. Hundreds of biblical passages describe God's own violent actions and commands to kill.

In the prophetic tradition Jesus rejected violence, oppression, and alienation. His life and teachings invited people into a new style of living, the Reign of God. Intimacy and trust, compassion and forgiveness, concern for justice and nonviolent love were key aspects of this new life.

The early followers of Jesus, as Wink points out, were not able to sustain the intensity of this revelation. In their attempts to make sense of Jesus' horrible death, some of the followers returned to the belief that violence saves. The God of mercy revealed by Jesus, Wink states, "was changed by the church into a wrathful God whose demand for blood atonement leads to God's requiring his own Son's death on behalf of us all" (*The Powers That Be*, p. 88).

Christianity's tradition, both in its theology and in the application to social and political issues (e.g., the just war theory), embodies this ancient tension between the unconditionally loving God revealed by Jesus and a god with traces of Marduk. In their ordinary convictions, many people reject Jesus' way of creative, active, nonviolent love as simply unrealistic, ignoring recent events worldwide in which nonviolence has worked. So they buy guns to protect and save, reaffirming once again the ancient belief in violence. Marduk is alive and well.

28

Wisdom Forged in Faith and Terrorism

How ought we respond to the horror of the September 11 terrorism and any future attacks?

From the very beginning I worried that the U.S. would respond with great force, slipping once again into the ancient belief that violence saves. The extensive use of war rhetoric only increased my fears. I sensed that columnists and editorials that sarcastically dismissed nonviolence and antiwar demonstrations were not offering sound guidance. I knew that justice was not vengeance.

I wondered if all those people, especially Christians, who were singing "God Bless America" really wanted to hear what God has already spoken about retaliation. During the week of the terrorist attack, the assigned readings for daily Eucharist were taken from Luke's Sermon on the Plain (6:17–49). On that Thursday we heard Jesus say: "But I say to you that listen, Love your enemies, do good to those who hate you, bless those who curse you, pray for those who abuse you. . . ."

During those days, the dominant response was still shock at the horrible evil and great grief. So I again turned to Scripture scholar Walter Wink, who writes in *Engaging the Powers*: "We are so interconnected with all of life that we cannot help being touched by the pain of all that suffers . . . . We human beings are far too frail and tiny to bear all this pain . . . . We are to articulate these agonizing longings and let them pass through us to God. Only the heart at the center of the universe can endure such a weight of suffering" (p. 305).

Recently, more insight into a proper response came from some U.S. Jesuits working in Peru. Given not only their faith but also their direct experience of terrorism over many years (parishes bombed, at least one of them captured by the "Shining Path" terrorists, much death and horror throughout Peru), they wrote to President Bush. With their permission, I share some of their thoughts. After expressing their horror and promising their prayers, they urge that those responsible for "these acts of evil" be brought to justice:

> Here in Peru it took us a long time to learn about the nature of terrorism and to find effective ways to struggle against it. We do not want the people of our native land to have to endure the same struggle of trial and error. We do not want our fellow countrymen and women to fall into the same trap of the vicious circle of violence breeding more violence . . . .
>
> Only when the terrorists could not demand support from the villagers did their campaign begin to decline. On the other hand, when the police and armed forces themselves used their military might for direct attacks against the terrorists in the rural communities, they created a situation which made the terrorists appear to be the better alternative.
>
> Terrorism is bred by ideological means, and it finds its ultimate justification in the poverty of the people who have no hope for a better life. Therefore, terrorism must be attacked on those same levels—by offering another 'ideology' to counteract the terrorist system and by responding to the root causes of violence.

The Jesuits go on to recommend three responses. First, the U.S. must begin massive "humanitarian programs," carefully monitored and using money originally budgeted for military attacks, to end the root causes of violence, especially for countries surrounding those that harbor terrorists (to let people "see that there are alternatives").

Second, the U.S. must use "all of its diplomatic efforts to pressure both Israel and the Palestinian movements to come to terms with each other in a definitive project of co-existence."

Third, Christian Churches in the U.S. must begin an "intensive program of interreligious dialogue in order to understand better what Islam really is."

The Jesuits' words of wisdom help us to discover how we can overcome evil without doing evil ourselves.

29

Praying for Peace

In the Eucharist, just after the Our Father, we pray for the gift of peace. Our prayer and simple gestures recall Jesus' encounter with his disciples on that first Easter evening (see John 20:19–23) and also express our need and desire for God's blessing today.

Having begun this year trapped in the cycle of violence, we surely long for the peace of Christ. The horror of terrorism and the continuing violent response capture attention—and cause death and destruction. Retaliation spills over into new violence in Israel and Palestine, in India and Pakistan. Ordinary violence, embedded in economic and social structures and accepted all too easily, damages and destroys life in homes, towns, nations around the globe.

In this darkness, Pope John Paul II speaks a word of hope. Inviting all people to begin the New Year with an urgent prayer for peace, the pope calls for a deeper understanding of peace. His title, "No Peace without Justice, No Justice without Forgiveness," accurately indicates the heart of the pope's challenging message. He writes: "I have often paused to reflect on the persistent question: how do we restore the moral and social order subjected to such horrific violence? My reasoned conviction, confirmed in turn by biblical revelation, is that the shattered order cannot be fully restored except by a response that combines justice with forgiveness. The pillars of true peace are justice and that form of love which is forgiveness."

The pope presents a sober analysis of the violence caused by organized terrorism, including the impact on the marginalized peoples in the developing world. He affirms the right to defend against terrorism, as long as this right is exercised in a legal and moral way. He also looks to the roots of terrorism: "International cooperation in the fight against terrorist activities must also include a courageous and resolute political, diplomatic and economic commitment to relieving situations of oppression and marginalization which facilitate the designs of terrorists."

As if anticipating our rejection of the possibility of forgiveness, John Paul states: "Forgiveness is not a proposal that can be immediately understood or easily accepted; in many ways it is a paradoxical message. Forgiveness, in fact, always involves an apparent short-term loss for a real long-term gain. Violence is the exact opposite; opting as it does for an apparent short-term gain, it involves a real and permanent loss. Forgiveness may seem like weakness, but it demands great spiritual strength and moral courage, both in granting it and in accepting it."

Pope John Paul's vision of peace will not be a popular one. For many people, the first and still dominant instinct, supported by political leaders and the media, is to wave the flag and drop the bombs. However, authentic peace, as John Paul indicates, only comes with justice and forgiveness. "No peace without justice, no justice without forgiveness: I shall not tire of repeating this warning to those who, for one reason or another, nourish feelings of hatred, a desire for revenge or the will to destroy."

How has and how will the pope's message influence your prayer for peace?

PART IV

Reproductive Technologies and Sexual Ethics

*Married couples should see it as their mission
to transmit human life and to educate their children;
they should realize that they are thereby cooperating with
the love of God the Creator and are, in a certain sense,
its interpreters. . . . But marriage was not instituted
solely for the procreation of children: its nature as an
indissoluble covenant between two people and the good
of the children demand that the mutual love of the partners
be properly expressed, that it should grow and mature.*

*The spiritual uneasiness of today and the changing structure
of life are part of a broader upheaval, whose symptoms
are the increasing part played on the intellectual level by
the mathematical, natural and human sciences and on the
practical level by their repercussions on technology.
The scientific mentality has brought about a change
in the cultural sphere and on habits of thought, and the
progress of technology is now reshaping the face of the earth.*

Pastoral Constitution on the Church in the Modern World, 50, 5

30

Reproductive Technologies: Questions

Cloning comes and goes from our headlines. But other headlines and stories frequently describe the promises and problems of other forms of reproductive technology—technological help in conceiving and bearing a child. Some time ago, a headline proclaimed: "Donated egg helps 63-year-old give birth."

Some years ago thousands of frozen embryos were destroyed in England because of a legal limit on storing frozen embryos. These fertilized eggs that are beginning human life were the "products" (this is the word from the newspaper account) of in vitro fertilization. Another story describes a sperm bank as a "donor-insemination service catering to heterosexual single women and lesbians." An advertisement in a national magazine announces that donor egg and in vitro fertilization services are "available now with no waiting list." A newspaper report tells of a woman using her dead husband's frozen sperm for artificial insemination.

What's going on here? A whole variety of means of reproduction offering hope to couples with infertility problems and to single people who desire to give birth. Along with these promises of hope, of course, come serious ethical questions!

Let's first consider some of the more common reproductive technologies. Artificial insemination makes use of the sperm of either the husband or a donor. The woman is inseminated with the help of technology, and fertilization (if it happens) occurs within the body of the woman. With in vitro fertilization the egg is fertilized in the glass dish and then transferred to the woman. In some cases, a surrogate mother enters the picture here—a person in whom implantation occurs and who eventually gives birth. The surrogate mother then gives the child to those who will parent the child. Surrogacy is based on a fee or on a simple agreement (for example, a woman has carried and given birth to her daughter's twins).

Methods, then, range from the relatively simple case of artificial insemination with the husband's sperm to the more complex situation of in vitro fertilization and surrogacy. Note that in this more complex situation four or five (or more) people can be involved in the conception, birth, and raising of the child: egg donor (a woman), sperm donor (a man), surrogate mother (a woman), those who then nurture and raise the child (a woman and a man, two women, two men, one man, one woman, etc.). A complex situation indeed!

Reproductive technologies raise many profound ethical questions, some of which I will wrestle with in the next chapter. For now, let's just start with some of the questions: Are there limits to what kind of technology (if any) can be used? Do persons have a right to have children? Can the desire to have a child "of one's own" become obsessive? What about third and fourth parties—the donors of sperm and egg? Is surrogacy ever justified? How do we make best use of scarce resources? What about unforeseen events—the deaths of the parents of frozen embryos, the change of partners, the surrogate mother who wants to keep the child?

What other questions does reproductive technology stir up in you?

~~ 31 ~~
Reproductive Technologies: Responses

Reproductive technology—artificial insemination, *in vitro* fertilization, surrogacy—raises profound ethical questions. In the last chapter, we mentioned both the various technologies and some of the questions. Now, let's look at some possible responses.

1. Many in our society say that it is up to the person or persons involved to determine whether reproductive technology is right or wrong. This ethical relativism in which each person determines morality may be appealing but finally is not a coherent and adequate ethical approach to making moral choices. The best of our Catholic tradition affirms a kind of objectivity or inbuilt meaning to our actions (and so to morality) which we together must come to discover—through the help of revelation along with the hard work of reasoning people. Always we search to do those actions which help life truly flourish.

2. The Vatican's Congregation for the Doctrine of the Faith gave its responses to reproductive technologies in its 1987 statement, "Instruction on Respect for Human Life in Its Origin and on the Dignity of Procreation: Replies to Certain Questions of the Day." (The main points are very briefly restated in the *Catechism*.) It begins by emphasizing the dignity of all human life and the meaning of marriage and procreation. When it turns to specific questions, the congregation judges that all the technologies that separate conception from sexual intercourse within marriage are morally wrong. The

basis for this judgment is the congregation's conviction that interfering with the biological process with its twin meanings of being unitive and procreative is wrong.

The statement also opposes all "third-party" involvement—a donor of egg or sperm or womb—for this violates the bond of marriage. The document condemns the destruction of all "spare" fertilized eggs (those not used for implanting), cloning, and nontherapeutic experimentation on embryos.

3. Some medical ethicists focus less on the use of technology and more on the meaning (reality) of the persons and relationships involved. From this perspective, artificial insemination with the husband's sperm can be understood in the context of a loving marriage. Technology appropriately assists the life-giving desires of the couple.

This focus on the meaning of persons also leads to serious questions about some aspects of reproductive technology. For example, many ethicists are concerned that such technology is transforming children (or potential children) into things, commodities to be manufactured according to certain specifications. People may forget that life is a gift of God, that we do not have absolute control over life, that we do not have a right to have a "child of one's own." Of course, loving people may have the best of intentions—but this does not necessarily justify all forms of reproductive technologies.

For this person-centered perspective, other threats to authentic human flourishing include surrogacy (a woman "renting" her womb) and the destruction of nonimplanted embryos (beginning human life). Other continuing questions include third-party involvement (could this be interpreted as very early adoption) and the best use of scarce resources (are there more pressing needs, as we remember our global interdependence).

Will you consider carefully the moral issues (including long-term implications) of artificial conception?

32

Cloning: A Blessing or a Curse?

A cute sheep by the name of Dolly caused a great uproar. Dolly came to be through the process of "cloning"—taking a cell from adult tissue, combining it with an unfertilized egg previously stripped of its genetic code, and eventually developing a new being. Dolly is genetically identical to the sheep from which the cell was taken, an exact copy. More recently, we were introduced to a cloned cat, dubbed Copy Cat.

Responses were immediate—and varied. Some recognized the positive potential of cloning for the study and treatment of genetic diseases. Others felt that the process had horrendous implications, especially for human beings. There was rhetoric about playing God and tampering with nature.

So, what can and ought Christian ethics say about cloning? First, two preliminary observations: (1) Ethical reflection must be based on clear understanding of what is happening—in this case, the process of cloning. (2) Rhetoric may stir people's reactions, but often it is not enlightening. In this case, charges of tampering with nature convey the individual's response to cloning. But in fact we often change or adapt nature. I wear glasses, for example, as many of you do, no doubt. We have used technology to change nature, to help us see better.

Christian ethics, then, must look calmly and carefully at the issue of cloning, understand exactly what is going on, and weigh honestly both the benefits and the risks. Surely there are potential benefits, especially in studying and then treating certain kinds of diseases. There are serious risks as well, some of which are about the impact of cloning (if it is applied to humans) on family and sexuality, on love and relationships. Christian ethics seeks to discover which action helps human life and all creation truly flourish.

In the case of cloning, many people see (and I find this insight convincing) that the greatest risk is actually undermining our humanity and that this risk far outweighs the benefits. What is meant by "undermining our humanity"? Damaging or destroying dimensions of human life that through our experience, reflection, and faith we have recognized as necessary for authentic life.

From a Christian perspective, we believe human beings to be sacred, to be images of God—not manufactured goods or merely a product of technology. Life belongs to God; we are to respect it and care for it, but we do not have absolute control over it. Would cloning cross this line? At least in some cases, it certainly would.

Other concerns that point to a rejection of cloning are related to justice questions, for example, who will make the decisions and why, and what role will "market forces" play? Will cloning lead to new possibilities of attempting to create a master race or to increasing the inequalities among peoples? Regulation will not control all abuses. We realize that if we *can* clone, we *will* do it, even though we *ought not* do it.

What moral concerns do Dolly and Copy Cat raise for you?

33

The Ethics of
Stem Cell Research

Whatever the president and congress decide about the federal funding of stem cell research, this complex scientific and public policy issue will continue to raise serious and sensitive ethical questions. So this chapter will briefly address three points. (1) What are stem cells? (2) What is the research? (3) What are the ethical dilemmas?

1. Stem cells are basic building blocks of the human being. They possess the ability to develop in any number of directions: a heart, a liver, a brain, etc. Some stem cells (called "totipotent") have the ability to develop into a complete human organism. Other stem cells (called "pluripotent") can develop into multiple cell types. As we grow, however, the cells become specialized—some make up the heart, others the brain, and so on.

2. Stem cells offer great potential for healing, including helping regenerate heart functions and treating diseases like Parkinson's and Alzheimer's. Not surprisingly, then, patient advocacy groups have joined many scientists in urging stem cell research to learn more about this potential.

3. The ethical dilemmas center not on the research as such but on the source of the stem cells (and on the steps necessary to obtain the cells). Much of the research so far has focused on embryos. In the early stages of development, the cells of a human embryo are stem cells. Harvesting the cells means destroying the embryo. Other

research makes use of stem cells found in umbilical cord blood and in bone marrow.

Clearly, then, the key ethical issue is the destruction of the embryo to obtain the stem cells.

What is an embryo? Simply "a collection of cells"? Or must we say more? The embryo is beginning human life with a unique genetic identity. It is not potential life; it is life with potential, needing only months of proper environment and nourishment to be born as a baby. Human life, then, deserves proper and appropriate respect (even if at the early stages the embryo may not yet be properly called a "person," because twinning is possible and we cannot split person-hood into two—each twin is a unique person).

Destruction of beginning human life contradicts and under-mines the value motivating the good cause of healing others, respect for life. Calling the process "life affirming" does not make it so. In this situation, there are clearly other alternatives, even if choosing the ethical path (using the other sources of stem cells) may mean going at a slower or less efficient pace in research.

Two more points. First, the fact that many of the embryos presently used in research are "leftovers" from fertility clinics does not change the morality of the act of destruction of the embryo. Rather, it raises the question of the morality of reproductive tech-nology, especially fertilizing more eggs (for financial reasons, among others) than will be implanted.

Second, the use of "leftovers" points to a fundamental moral problem in the whole area: undermining our humanness by trans-forming human life into things. Notice the language: people "make" and "use" embryos; they "experiment" on them and "discard" them. Beginning human life is no longer an awesome gift of God but a product of our hands.

34

Stem Cells, Solidarity, and Social Justice

I n the last chapter, I addressed the moral question at the center of embryonic stem cell research: the destruction of the embryo in order to harvest the stem cells. In this chapter, I want to focus on the wider context that includes profound moral dilemmas often overlooked. Two in particular: the technological threat to our humanness and the demands of social justice.

Because of space limitations, I was able only to mention briefly in my last chapter the threat to our humanness. Our advances in technology are truly wonderful but also problematic, especially with various forms of reproductive technology. The wonderful part is technology's capacity to help resolve and heal difficult and painful conditions. The problematic part is that the momentum of technological advance risks undermining our humanness. We make persons into things, human life into a commodity. A recent cartoon by Jim Borgman expressed it perfectly: the woman was ordering on the phone from "The Genome Barn" catalog. She said, "Yes, I'd like to order item number 94773-B, the do-it-yourself chromosome manipulation makeover kit with the cloning adaptor. . . . Oh, and, what the heck, a set of frozen identical twins, in blonde."

The second moral issue, not mentioned at all in the preceding chapter, is the just use of resources. Our country (indeed, the world) does not have the time, talent, and treasure to do everything we need to do, much less everything we want to do. So priorities must be determined. Catholic teaching has long stressed the importance of the universal common good, so our vision must be very wide!

This social justice perspective includes concerns about where resources are spent: one recent article mentioned that only a few companies hold many of the patents in this area—the potential for profit is enormous. Another concern is who benefits from the results, in a country where millions do not have medical insurance and in a world where the gap between the "haves" and the "have-nots" is increasing.

Many U.S. citizens, including the present administration, apparently do not want to consider the moral implications of many systemic issues, especially economic ones. However, the long social justice tradition that includes the prophets and Jesus calls us to face these challenges.

In a word, we must consider investing more of our resources as a society in research related to urgent and more basic needs, such as worldwide hunger.

This may sound harsh to those who are suffering from diseases possibly helped by stem cell research. Surely it is not meant to be that—my father died from Lou Gehrig's disease, a debilitating disease that research has not yet solved. It is meant to stretch our U.S. vision to include the hundreds of millions of our sisters and brothers who not only face many diseases but also have little food and clean water.

Once again we see the need for a bold proclamation of the consistent ethic of life. Being pro-life ranges from the tiny embryo to the global economy. This debate about stem cells reminds us of the blessings and the threats of our technological age.

How will you choose life?

35

Sexual Ethics
and American Culture

I have often postponed writing about this topic. Why? Because
ethics in our society, perhaps especially sexual ethics, is
profoundly influenced by relativism. Because sexuality in our society
has been trivialized by TV, movies, and advertising. Because the credibility of celibate males regarding sexual ethics is questioned by many.

So, even though there is a pressing need for prayerful reflection
on and discussion of sexual ethics, who wants to walk into such a
hornet's nest!

Then two sentences from a respectable national magazine caught
my attention. The first sentence, in an article about television,
described why some men want to go to bed with two women at
once. The second sentence, in an article about medical research,
described an individual who had had between two thousand and
three thousand sexual partners.

Evidently, something is terribly wrong. Despite the hornet's nest,
we *must* enter into the prayerful reflection and discussion.

First, a few thoughts about our culture as the context for this
reflection. Ethical relativism emphasizes that the individual's
decision makes the act wrong or right. "Each person must decide for
himself or herself." Relativism does not acknowledge a kind of objectivity in moral dilemmas, a meaning rooted in our shared humanity.
The many ways our media make sexuality into a commodity or
glorify casual sex are evident to most people—just think of commer-
cials and sitcoms, for example.

The long history of the Catholic Church's teaching about sexuality has included numerous negative views, including denying the goodness of sex and degrading the dignity of women. Still, the teaching has attempted to hold together sex with love, love with marriage, marriage with children. But not until the Second Vatican Council were the unitive and procreative dimensions of sexual intercourse equally valued.

We ought not be surprised, given both the pervasive power of cultural influences and this checkered history of sexual ethics, that credibility is questioned.

What, then, is the heart of Catholic sexual ethics? Sexual intercourse is understood to be both unitive and procreative, that is, it expresses and deepens the relationship of the two people and is open to new life. Given this meaning, which is discovered by paying attention to human experience and by listening to revelation and tradition (we are not free to say sexual intercourse means whatever we want it to mean—this is what ethical relativism does), the official Church teaches that sex can find authentic expression only within the permanent commitment of marriage. This loving and equal partnership provides the context for the couple's love to grow and to be embodied in children.

Sexual expression is a profound body language, communicating the deepest thoughts and feelings, indeed, the very self. It deserves a proper context, proper respect. We are very aware of the many ways this unique form of communication is violated, with devastating results: sexually transmitted diseases, teenage pregnancies, abortions, broken spirits and broken families, abuse of all kinds.

Continuing questions in sexual ethics focus not only on the primacy of the loving partnership as the context for all moral reflection but also on a number of specific issues such as homosexuality and reproductive technologies.

How do our cultural messages about sexuality, your desire to live as a faithful disciple of Jesus, church teachings, and your own experience fit together in your life?

⌇ 36 ⌇

Homosexuality

The American bishops have directed our attention to the topic of homosexuality. The Committee on Marriage and Family of the National Conference of Catholic Bishops issued "Always Our Children: A Pastoral Message to Parents of Homosexual Children and Suggestions for Pastoral Ministers" (*Origins*, October 9, 1997). Stephen J. Rossetti and Gerald D. Coleman contributed additional insights in their article "Psychology and the Church's Teaching on Homosexuality" (*America*, November 1, 1997). These two publications are encouraging and enlightening. Responses to the articles highlight continuing questions.

The bishops' statement seeks to offer pastoral guidance, and so only summarizes key aspects of the Church's teaching as a foundation for its comments. Central to this teaching is the distinction between homosexual orientation and homosexual behavior. Homosexual orientation, the emotional and sexual attraction toward individuals of the same sex, is generally experienced as a given and not as something freely chosen—and so is not an issue of morality. Many experts conclude that genetic, hormonal, and psychological factors lead to this orientation.

Homosexual behavior is judged objectively immoral because it contradicts the meaning of sexual intercourse. The bishops restate the Catholic tradition: "Only within marriage does sexual intercourse fully symbolize the Creator's dual design as an act of covenant love with the potential of co-creating new human life." Genital sexual expression is to be unitive and procreative, love-giving and life-giving.

Other important points in the statement include: (1) an emphasis on the whole person; total personhood is more than just one's sexuality; (2) everyone is created in God's image, and so has inherent dignity; (3) all forms of discrimination, from humor to violence, must be stopped; "nothing in the Bible or in Catholic teaching can be used to justify prejudicial or discriminatory attitudes and behavior"; (4) sensitivity to the range of feelings of parents, encouragement to love and support homosexual children, a list of pastoral recommendations for families and church ministers.

The article on psychology presents the Church's teaching, stresses the appropriate roles for the science of psychology, and affirms that Catholic psychologists can both follow church teachings and work with personal integrity in their own field of expertise. Other significant topics in this article are the origin of homosexuality, the question whether it is a disorder, the problem of homophobia, and attempts to change one's orientation.

Responses, of course, have been varied. One thoughtful, though certainly not new, position asks whether it is right to require celibacy of all homosexuals. Homosexuals can and do form faithful, exclusive, and permanent relationships. Could not these relationships be considered love-giving and life-giving in some real if analogous way? Are the Church's laws too biologically focused, instead of considering the whole person? Do the passages in the Bible concerning homosexuality reflect cultural fear and prejudice more than divine revelation? Profound questions, indeed, which call for continued careful reflection on tradition and experience and for respectful listening and dialogue.

Do you experience any prejudices toward gays and lesbians? What is your reaction to the teaching and to the questions?

~~ 37 ~~

Divorce, Remarriage, and the Eucharist

A moral dilemma which has long troubled many persons concerns divorce, remarriage, and reception of the Eucharist. Misunderstandings, pain, and profound questions surround these complex issues, which touch the lives of so many families. The epidemic of divorce and the desire to respond pastorally to the divorced and remarried have highlighted the urgency to reflect carefully on church teachings and responses.

The *Catechism of the Catholic Church* (Libreria Editrice Vaticana, 1997, 1994) presents the official teaching about divorce and communion (1650; see also 1638–1651): "In fidelity to the words of Jesus Christ . . . the Church maintains that a new union cannot be recognized as valid, if the first marriage was. If the divorced are remarried civilly, they find themselves in a situation that objectively contravenes God's law. Consequently, they cannot receive Eucharistic communion as long as this situation persists."

Common misunderstandings about this teaching need to be corrected. A divorced person is not excommunicated; a divorced person (who has not remarried) is not barred from receiving the sacraments. A divorced person who has remarried (without the first marriage being annulled—an annulment is a judgment made by a church court that a sacramental marriage never actually existed) is not excommunicated, but remains a member of the Church, although not allowed by law to receive communion.

Many members of the Church, including bishops, have been searching for appropriate pastoral responses. Others also see the need to address fundamental theological questions, such as What is the moral obligation stemming from a failed first marriage? What a challenging task this is—to remain faithful to Jesus' vision of permanence; to respect church teaching and also acknowledge the possibility of and need for revision (as in the post-Vatican II emphasis on marriage as a covenant and not just a contract); to take seriously the painful experience of good and faithful people.

To help this process of searching, Kenneth Himes, O.F.M., and James Coriden have offered several points. (Please see their article, "Notes on Moral Theology," in *Theological Studies*, March, 1996, for more details and many references.) (1) The model of marriage as covenant emphasizes the loving partnership in all aspects of life—spiritual, emotional, psychological, financial, etc. Church teaching ought not to focus only on the sexual dimension. (2) Sin may be involved in the divorce, that is, in the destruction of the loving community of marriage. Repentance for this sin is necessary. And then participation in the Eucharist would be possible. Remarriage, they suggest, may be understood in a similar way. (3) Concerning the Eucharist itself, the authors point out that the sacraments both celebrate what is already fulfilled and bring about what they celebrate. Or, put another way, sacraments are not "rewards for a life well lived but a means to deepen one's love of God and desire for conversion."

Some people may judge that the suggestions of Himes and Coriden stretch official teaching too much. But surely their call for a serious and in-depth dialogue seems justified by the searching and suffering in so many lives.

How has this complex dilemma impacted your life or the lives of family and friends?

38

HIV / AIDS

S ome time ago, a front-page headline stated: "AIDS deaths drop 47%." It spoke the truth, giving us good news indeed—but not the whole truth. Only if we read the entire article did we learn three other parts of the truth: (1) The spread of HIV, the virus that causes AIDS, has not dropped; (2) some researchers worry that the new drug combinations, the cause for the decline in deaths, will stop working; (3) in the developing world where 90 percent of all HIV-infected people live, there is no possibility of using these very expensive therapies.

I wonder how many people missed the whole truth. Could reading just the headline reinforce the mistaken judgment that HIV/AIDS no longer need be a great concern? Indeed, there seems to be a growing sense in our country, inspired by the present success of the drug therapies, that we have taken care of AIDS. Or could it be that we as the public have become numb to the suffering, especially among minority groups and in the developing countries? Or, worse yet, that we have deliberately turned away from these people?

To refocus on the whole truth and to find one concrete way to contribute would be an appropriate way to begin our response to the crisis. Let's start right now with a brief review about the basics of HIV/AIDS.

AIDS (Acquired Immune Deficiency Syndrome) is caused by HIV (Human Immunodeficiency Virus). This virus attacks certain white blood cells, eventually destroying the person's immune system. Once infected, a person is able to infect other persons, even though the infected person shows no signs of the disease (this is why the rate of infection has not dropped). The AIDS virus is spread in several ways: sexual contact (including heterosexual and homosexual intercourse), exchange of blood (especially by sharing needles for drugs), and the birth process (an infected mother can transmit the virus to her infant). HIV is not spread through casual contact, such as hugging or sneezing.

It is estimated that more than 34 million people are infected; of the adults more than 40 percent are women. Every day, seven thousand young people (aged ten to twenty-four) are infected with HIV. Researchers also estimate that more than 70 percent of all infections are attributed to heterosexual intercourse.

Nations already reeling from poverty, famine, war, and other diseases are being overwhelmed by AIDS. Wherever HIV enters a population, it always moves to those peoples who are already experiencing poverty, oppression, alienation, and marginalization. The harsh reality of HIV/AIDS, then, cries out for individual and systemic responses.

What can you do? Start by learning more about the whole truth of HIV/AIDS. Then perhaps you can help your parish do that too. Education and prevention are still the key; groups in the city and diocese can help you plan a program. You can also give some of your time (or at least money) to one of these agencies or to national ones. Tackling the systemic issues that contribute to the spread of HIV—racism, lack of education, oppression of women, and poverty—will be more effective through organized efforts.

What first step will you take?

PART V

End-of-Life Ethics

It is when faced with death that the enigma of the human condition is most evident. People are tormented not only by pain and by the gradual diminution of their bodily powers but also, and even more, by the dread of forever ceasing to be. But a deep instinct leads them rightly to shrink from and to reject the utter ruin and total loss of their personality. Because they bear in themselves the seed of eternity, which cannot be reduced to mere matter, they rebel against death. All the helps made available by technology, however useful they may be, cannot set their anguished minds at rest. They may prolong their lifespan; but this does not satisfy their heartfelt longing, one that can never be stifled, for an afterlife.

While the imagination is at a loss before the mystery of death, the church, taught by divine revelation, declares that God has created people in view of a blessed destiny that lies beyond the boundaries of earthly misery.

Pastoral Constitution on the Church in the Modern World, 18

~~ 39 ~~

The Death Penalty

A photo in a newspaper showed a group of people celebrating with champagne the execution of a criminal. Most of us probably would not join such a demonstration; yet, according to recent polls, 70 percent of us (U.S. citizens) favor the death penalty.

Still, the Catholic bishops of the United States have consistently called for the abolition of the death penalty. In their statement *Capital Punishment* (1980), the bishops carefully explain their pro-life position. The bishops stress the unique worth and dignity of every person and the belief that God alone is the Lord of life. The bishops recognize that crime is often rooted in complex social conditions of poverty and injustice, and so call for more attention to correcting the root causes of crime than to enlarging death row. They acknowledge that abortion, euthanasia, and the death penalty are not the same issue, but each topic points to the same fundamental value: safeguarding the sanctity of life.

More than debate about deterrence and retribution (traditional reasons for supporting the death penalty), more than social analysis, the bishops' position on capital punishment embodies and expresses commitment to the Gospel. Quite simply, "we believe that abolition of the death penalty is most consonant with the example of Jesus." The God revealed in the life of Jesus is a God of forgiveness and redemption, of love and compassion—in a word, a God of life.

Gut-level reactions may cry out for vengeance, but Jesus' example in the Gospels invites all of us to develop a new and different attitude toward violence. The bishops encourage us to embody Jesus' message in practical and civic decisions.

Of course, society must protect itself. Imprisonment will be necessary, but ought not to dehumanize the convicts. (This raises another issue: the reform of the prison system to make it conducive to rehabilitation.) Also, special concern and care must be given to victims and to the families of victims.

Despite the message of Jesus and the teachings of our religious leaders, many people are still caught up in the anger and outrage over violent crime. In one sense, this rage is understandable. But it cannot remain one's final position, for it will dehumanize all who hold fast to it. Recall those people celebrating an execution with champagne. People who retain an attitude of revenge and vindictiveness are tormented and embittered, empty and unhealed.

Such a judgment comes from one who has been there—Marietta Jaeger Lane. Her seven-year-old daughter, Susie, was kidnapped and murdered. Now Marietta works with Murder Victims' Families for Reconciliation, urging us to move past fears and political rhetoric to a consistent ethic of life. Her story and the film *Dead Man Walking* (about Sister Helen Prejean's death row ministry) remind us that the ideal can be lived in the real world.

Many people support the death penalty without really thinking about its moral implications. Will you be open to new thoughts and feelings, open to be challenged by the Church's pro-life message about the death penalty?

～ 40 ～

Murder / Suicide
Among the Elderly

A chilling article appeared in the local paper some time ago. Just as startling was the response of a group of high school students.

The article discussed the increase of suicide and murder among the elderly. Several tragic events in the Cincinnati area led reporter Julie Irwin to find research about such occurrences. Donna Cohen's study of 60 murder-suicides among elderly couples in Florida from 1988 to 1994 revealed these facts: 100 percent were committed by men; 96 percent took place in the home; 95 percent involved guns; 40 percent of the husbands appeared to suffer from depression. Although 50 percent of the wives had suffered a general decline in health, about 67 percent had indicated that they did not want to die.

Startling—and the source of many questions! Why do we so easily turn to violence as a response to a difficult situation? Why are the "we" so often men—100 percent in this study? Why are guns so available? Why is there a breakdown in medical care and social support? Why isn't there more concern that men between 75 and 84 have the highest suicide rate in the United States? Why is euthanasia ("mercy killing") becoming more and more acceptable in our country?

All of these questions, of course, have profound ethical dimensions. Our Church has addressed many of them: calling us to create a culture of life, endorsing gun control, urging welfare and health-care reform that pays special attention to the poor and elderly, opposing euthanasia, spelling out when medical treatment need not be used, reminding people of the usefulness of living wills and the durable power of attorney for health care. (In the next few chapters, I will discuss some of these topics in more detail.)

The high school students? While discussing the meaning and application of Christian ethics with them, I presented a case of an elderly man killing his ailing wife. Their response? One said, "It's up to the old man to decide if it was right or wrong." Another added, "What does religion have to do with this anyway?" In my response, I pointed out—without much success—that actions have meaning and consequences beyond our intentions. Shooting someone is not an act of mercy just because I say it is or want it to be. The task of Christian ethics is to discover and consider all the relevant aspects of the case. Even after many years of Catholic education, however, the students expressed the relativism and individualism of our culture and not the morality of the Gospel.

Tragic death, research, a high school classroom: so very different yet curiously intertwined. What does this trio mean for all of us? Certainly it leads us to consider the questions and the Church's guidance, to reflect on what values we hand on to younger generations. It also leads us to care concretely for the elderly, helping them get proper medical treatment and offering support and love. It may also mean—if you are elderly—being willing to reach out for help.

Who in your life needs your care this week?

～～ 41 ～～

Euthanasia and the Bible

End-of-life issues touch the depths of our being, stir the emotions, and raise profound questions—and so call for careful moral reasoning.

We hear about alarming rates of murder/suicide among the elderly. Jack Kevorkian helped many people commit suicide. Physicians and ethicists publish careful guidelines for permitting euthanasia ("mercy killing"). Magazines and television shows subtly support the "right-to-die." States have attempted to pass laws legalizing physician-assisted suicide and euthanasia (and surely more states will follow).

How can we respond to these troubling and tragic events and to the underlying issues? We begin by acknowledging the pain and mystery of suffering and dying. And by admitting the fears: fear of being a burden on one's family, fear of unbearable pain, fear of exhausting one's savings, fear of prolonging death with tubes and machines.

Then we can turn to the Bible which provides a sound foundation and sure direction as we wrestle with these complex issues and fears. Two points emerge from the Scriptures.

First, we appreciate that life is a basic good. In Genesis we hear of the sacredness of human life which is deserving of respect and reverence. In Jesus, we see how God so cherished humanity as to become one of us. In Paul's First Letter to the Corinthians, we read: "For God's temple is holy, and you are that temple" (1 Corinthians 3:17b).

Second, we are to be stewards of life, but we do not have complete control. Stewardship implies that we have the responsibility to care for something that is not totally our own possession. As the bishops of Ohio wrote in *Hopes and Fears: Pastoral Reflections of Death* (1993): "Because we have been fashioned in the image of the Creator, we are, in a sense, 'co-creators.'"

These biblically rooted convictions are basic to our opposition to euthanasia. We use our creativity to cure illness and promote wellness. We respond with care and compassion to those who are suffering. (Indeed, we have much to learn about better methods of pain control.) Mercy killing, however, moves beyond stewardship. Euthanasia, even for compassionate reasons, implies that we have absolute control over life and so contradicts who we are as "co-creators."

The same reasons apply to assisted suicide. Recognizing both the good gift of life and our responsibilities as stewards prohibits choosing suicide or helping someone else to end his or her life. Suicide, though rooted in pain and despair, is an attempt to seize ultimate control over life. It contradicts the fundamental reality of our lives.

As we discuss euthanasia and assisted suicide in terms of public policy, other reasons must also be given. Many are convinced that legalizing euthanasia would further undermine reverence for life in our society, would reduce trust in the medical profession, and would put old and infirm people in vulnerable positions.

Euthanasia evokes powerful emotions and may seem to be merciful when sincere persons desire to help suffering people. Our Scriptures point in a different direction. We must not kill, but instead be present with care and compassion.

Have you prayerfully and thoughtfully considered the moral dimensions of euthanasia and assisted suicide?

~ 42 ~

Withdrawal of Life Support

Have you ever said to your family, "Don't put me on all those life-support machines and tubes"? Perhaps you had just visited a friend dying in the hospital, or were simply reacting to well-publicized stories, such as those about Karen Quinlan and Nancy Cruzan.

Perhaps you know someone who has already agonized over making such a decision. Or have wondered how this is different from euthanasia.

So, what does the Church say about withholding or withdrawing various life-support measures? Actually, there is a long tradition dealing with this issue, dating back hundreds of years. Technology has certainly changed since then, but the principles can still enlighten our decisions!

The tradition is rooted in the Bible, which tells us that life is a fundamental but not absolute good. (We would not, for example, destroy our relationship with God through sin in order to save our physical life.) Also we understand death in the context of belief in new life. Our belief in everlasting life is rooted in the transforming experience of the resurrection of Jesus.

The Christian tradition provides this guidance about the use of life-support measures: ordinary means must be used; extraordinary means are optional. Ordinary means are interventions that offer reasonable hope of benefit and can be used without excessive expense, pain, or other inconvenience.

It is important to remember that "ordinary" and "extraordinary" refer not just to the technology but to the treatment in relation to the condition of the patient, in other words, the relative proportion of benefit and burden the treatment provides the patient (see the Vatican's *Declaration on Euthanasia*, section IV [1980]).

Within the Catholic Church, debate still surrounds the question of withdrawing artificial nutrition and hydration. While one position holds that medical nourishment must be provided in almost all cases, another position asks what possibility the sick person has for pursuing life's purposes—happiness, fulfillment, love of God and neighbor—when discerning whether the life-support can be removed. If a fatal disease or condition is present and if life-prolonging efforts would be useless or a severe burden in pursuing life's purposes, then we can withdraw the feeding tubes and allow the person to die as a result of the fatal disease or condition. This position strongly opposes euthanasia, affirms the individual's right to be the primary decision maker, and stresses the moral distinction between allowing a person to die and killing that person.

Clearly, such a decision could be made only after extensive consultation with medical, nursing, and pastoral care staffs. Communication is of utmost importance—with one's family also, where friction or guilt feelings about relationships frequently cause difficulties. This is especially true when someone must make the decision for the patient who is too sick to decide.

Human life is a gift from God deserving respect and care. Our Catholic tradition, however, tells us that we do not have to do every-thing possible in every situation to keep ourselves or someone else alive.

As a believer in the Resurrection, can you trust that death marks the transition to new and transformed life?

~ 43 ~

Advance Directives

A s we wrestle with end-of-life issues such as euthanasia or with-drawal of life-support systems, is there anything else we can do *now?* Yes! We can fill out an *advance directive*, that is, a form explaining our wishes concerning future health care.

One type of advance directive is a *living will*. This form is a statement prepared in advance so that people, while competent, can direct their families and physicians concerning the type of treatment they want or do not want if they become terminally ill and are no longer able to express their desires about medical treatment.

The living will, because it is filled out in advance, can never foresee all the details of a future illness and the related medical procedures. This is its major limitation. On the other hand, it gives evidence of reflection and desires concerning what kind of treatment the person wants.

A second type of advance directive is the *durable power of attorney for health care* (also called "health care surrogate" or "proxy" but different from "power of attorney"). In this document an indi-vidual gives another person the legal authority to make health-care decisions when the individual is no longer able to do so. The decisions made by the appointed person are based on the current medical condition of the patient and on the patient's previously expressed desires concerning treatment. As a result, this form of dealing with dying-and-death situations seems to be preferable. It does not rely merely on a previously written statement to cover all possible situations.

In appointing someone to act on your behalf, clearly choose someone you trust, someone with whom you have carefully discussed your wishes concerning treatment. After you have completed the form, give a copy to the appointed person, to your physician, to someone in your family, and to your local pastor. Your lawyer or physician can provide the proper form for you. Besides creating a legal document, the process is just as important for the communication (with the appointed person, with your physician, with your family) which is a necessary part. The time for this discussion and appointing is *now*—and not at a time of crisis. Also, this process is necessary for all of us, whatever our age; it is not just for senior citizens.

All this may seem like too much effort. It is not! The whole process of planning now for the hour of death is a concrete way to express your care and love for your family and friends, since they will be the ones faced with the difficult and painful decisions. It is a way to relieve fears of a prolonged dying by being attached needlessly to machines. It is a way to counteract the movement toward euthanasia. It is a way to express your concern for the appropriate use of the earth's limited resources. Finally, such planning can also be a prayerful experience, confronting the final mystery of life and trusting in our gracious God.

What concrete steps will you take to plan now for the hour of death?

44

Assisted Suicide
and the Supreme Court

The 1997 Supreme Court decision concerning assisted suicide calls for caution and commitment rather than celebration.

The Supreme Court did not ban assisted suicide forever; it simply stated that assisted suicide is not a constitutional right. There is some small room for celebration here: at least the court did not repeat the mistake of the abortion decision, sweeping away all laws and debate and creating a right. Instead, the court concluded that the discussion about assisted suicide should continue, especially at the level of state legislatures and referenda. States can ban assisted suicide, but they can also legalize it.

Thus, the need for caution; the court's ruling has not settled the issue of euthanasia but only encouraged the democratic discussion of the topic. Two other points to note: (1) polls consistently show that a majority of U.S. citizens favor euthanasia and assisted suicide; (2) some of the Supreme Court justices indicated an openness to accepting legalized assisted suicide in certain circumstances. The whole debate remains in its first stages. There will continue to be lots of pressure to legalize euthanasia.

And so the need for commitment. I would like to suggest three areas: (1) understanding, (2) the legal debate, (3) religious convictions.

Understanding: Those of us who are opposed to euthanasia and assisted suicide must do our homework carefully so that we can express our position clearly. We must understand the difference between "killing" and "allowing to die," between "ethically ordinary" means of life support and "ethically extraordinary." We also need to know the "why" that drives the euthanasia movement, including real suffering and fears; so we pay attention to better treatment of pain and proper use of hospice care. We must find ways to work with others who oppose assisted suicide but do not share our religious convictions.

The legal debate: As citizens we must get involved in the discussion that undoubtedly will be emotional, tense, even bitter. We must shape laws that help build a culture of life. Here especially a nuanced understanding is important, for some Catholic groups with good intentions actually make the process more complicated by pushing positions that contradict the Church's long tradition on allowing a person to die (the Church has consistently taught that we do not have to do "everything possible" to keep a person alive).

Religious convictions: Because we live in a democratic society, some laws of the land may not reflect our religious values. Abortion and capital punishment are just two examples. Someday, legalized euthanasia and assisted suicide may be another. So we must remember that what is legal may not be moral; legality is sometimes distinct from morality. Whatever the law of the land, as disciples of Jesus, we must nourish and hand on our religious convictions, for example, about the dignity of all persons and about care and compassion for those in need. Especially when our society gives us different messages, we must tell our great story of Jesus and actively participate in communities of faith, celebration, and action.

What do you need in order to nourish your commitment for the long haul?

45

Life with All the Saints

When Aunt Rita died, she was almost ninety-six, the last of her generation in our family. After her brother and sister died, my two brothers, sisters-in-law, their families, and I were all the family she had. Rita, the only aunt I ever really knew, was also my godmother.

For the last year and a half, she lived in assisted living, receiving excellent care. But it wasn't like her home—where she had lived for more than ninety years (yes, in the same house). For quite some time, Rita dearly desired to go home to God. But it wasn't her time, a fact that she wasn't very patient about!

Then several weeks before her death Aunt Rita had a stroke and her condition declined steadily. We were faced with the questions of life-support systems (legally, I had durable power of attorney for health care). Fortunately, Rita made her desires very clear in recent years: no extraordinary means. Still, I felt the subtle pressures from well-intentioned health care personnel who wanted to treat Rita more aggressively. Even more, I felt the pain of Rita's slow decline toward death. Even with good care and later help from hospice, Rita seemed to struggle in some way, wanting to die yet holding on to life.

One day, after visiting Rita and discussing her condition with her nurses, I said to my brother, "I am really feeling the powerful emotional pull of the argument for euthanasia. Rita will surely die; why make her go through this struggle?" Many of us have heard some form of this argument: Wouldn't it be the merciful thing to do to end the person's suffering? He knew, of course, that I am opposed to euthanasia and assisted suicide. I still am.

This experience, however, reminded me of important lessons. The emotional appeal "to be merciful" can be very seductive. We ought not to underestimate the persuasive power of this appeal either in making end-of-life decisions or in formulating state laws. We must, then, find ways to nourish and share our conviction that we are stewards of life: we care for the gift of life, but we do not have absolute control over life. To kill would contradict who we are as images of God, "co-creators" as the Ohio bishops have said. Even if we have only the purest of intentions, this contradiction still exists.

My family and I waited with Aunt Rita, trying to calm the struggle, praying. Finally, she died. What a profound mystery is life and suffering, death and new life!

Song and music were some of Rita's favorite things. Also, she worked in the cafeteria of a local high school for more than thirty years. Of course, she always served us tasty meals too! So, her funeral Mass focused on song and food, which just happen to be favorite images in the Scriptures for describing life after death as a wonderful banquet.

Rita has gone home to God—just in time for a special feast, now her feast too. So, Aunt Rita, enjoy the eternal banquet with all the saints!

Catholic Morality: Has It Changed?

The teenagers in a Catholic high school say, "It's up to the old man to decide if it was right or wrong to kill his wife suffering from Alzheimer's disease."

In a parish adult-ed class, an older woman states, "Just do what God tells us; just follow the Church's laws. What's all this worry about mature moral decision making?"

Very different views, aren't they? You too have probably wrestled with moral dilemmas: "Why be faithful to my spouse?" Or "Why should I try to live a moral life in the first place? Other people don't seem to care and yet they are happy and make lots of money." Stop for a moment to reflect on just *how* you come to moral decisions. Along the way, maybe you also have wondered why the pope and bishops seem to be getting involved in politics and economics.

All this leads us to ask: What has happened to Catholic morality? In the years since Vatican II, there have been so many changes. Some people call it renewal; others claim the Church has gotten soft or confused; still others emphasize the profound impact that a consumer society can have on our personal lives.

In this appendix I will sort through the confusion, highlighting changes from the older morality to the new and considering the influence our culture has on our moral decision making.

A LOOK BACK

Christianity, of course, has always provided guidance for people's actions. Through the centuries, the Church has developed not only laws but also ways to help people make moral decisions. Those of us who grew up in the pre-Vatican II Church experienced a particular style of morality. Those of you who are old enough will recall how this morality worked and felt—and probably can tell stories both amusing and tragic. For those of you who do not remember this type of morality, here is a brief summary.

Morality, at least as it was experienced by ordinary people, was usually closely connected with confession. We reviewed the Ten Commandments and church laws to see which ones we broke. That was sin. Of course we knew that sin offended God, but breaking the law was more often the real focus. The laws provided crystal-clear guidance: when faced with a moral question, just find the right law and follow it. And, although it probably was never said this explicitly, many of us believed that if we followed the law, we would earn our way into heaven. God "owed" us salvation if we did the right thing. Breaking the law in a serious way, mortal sin, would lead to hell.

Although Catholic social teaching already had quite a history, the most important issue in the popular mind was sexuality. Conscience was always discussed and respected, but the impression was given that the properly formed conscience would always follow church teaching and laws exactly.

The clergy's training in morality also focused on confession. Priests were taught how to help people distinguish between mortal and venial sins. While many people encountered compassionate confessors, many of those amusing and tragic stories also come from the confessional.

The theory grounding this education was a philosophical understanding of human beings which is called the "natural law." God's law, this theory held, was written in human nature. By understanding human nature properly, we could spell out the laws needed to direct our actions. For example, our ability to speak is linked to human communication and therefore to laws about the need for honesty and truth telling. Similarly, sexual intercourse is linked to procreation and so to laws about the use of contraceptives.

This pre-Vatican II style of morality possessed a power and clarity that directed people's lives. Law and obedience were key characteristics, even though these could, and did, slip into rigidity and authoritarianism. People had a sense of the why, what, and how of Catholic morality. Why: to serve God and to avoid punishment (fear of hell!). What: the content of the laws spelled out by church leaders about many areas of life, especially sexuality. How: obedience and duty to law and authority.

Let's return to our opening scenes: this style of morality would be utterly foreign to those teenagers in the Catholic high school. It would feel like an unfair limiting of their freedom. The teenagers' understanding and reactions, by the way, are almost certainly rooted not in the renewal of Catholic morality but in the powerful messages of our materialistic society (we will return to this point).

On the other hand, the older woman in the parish would feel completely comfortable with this pre-Vatican II morality. It is clear, simple, secure; it is what she is recommending. Well, almost. Society has had its impact on her as well. On some topics she does not follow the guidance of the pope and the bishops, mostly issues related to politics and economics. She supports the death penalty, for example, and is suspicious of the U.S. bishops' positions expressed in their pastoral letter *Economic Justice for All*.

VATICAN II'S RENEWAL

The negative elements embedded in the pre-Vatican II style of morality—its distance from Scripture, its static view of the world, its rigidity and emphasis on obedience—gradually led people to recognize the need for renewal. First, scholars in moral theology, Scripture, and other areas of theology began planting seeds of change by their study and writings.

Then, the bishops of Vatican II made this renewal of Catholic morality an essential part of the overall renewal and reform of the Church: "Special attention needs to be given to the development of moral theology" (*On Priestly Formation,* 16). In their own documents, especially in the *Pastoral Constitution on the Church in the Modern World,* they gave direction for this development: the use of Scripture, the acceptance of a worldview open to change, the role of the laity, deep respect for conscience, concern for political and economic issues.

Most importantly, the renewal turned from philosophy to Scripture for the foundation and center of morality. The life and teachings of Jesus, the meaning of being created in God's image and called into covenant, the rich imagination and challenge of the prophets, the cost of discipleship, the hope and vision of being an Easter people—all this provided the basis for understanding the why and what of Catholic morality. God's revelation guides us in understanding who we are and how we are to act.

The reform of moral theology also turned from the earlier view of the natural law which emphasizes the unchangeable, the abstract, the universal to a more modern view which understands life as historical and developing, concrete and particular. Following the lead of Pope John XXIII and the council, moral theologians read carefully "the signs of the time" and paid attention to the joys and hopes, the grief and anguish of people around the world. Morality deals with real people in a great variety of cultures with need of liberation in many forms, both personal and political.

The Vatican II bishops had expressed great respect for conscience, especially in their declaration on religious liberty. This emphasis and respect, however, was seriously tested only a few years after Vatican II—in the debate over birth control and Pope Paul VI's encyclical *Humanae Vitae*. Widespread disagreement marked the response to the encyclical, some people calling for strict agreement, others appealing to conscience which could be well-informed and in disagreement with the pope.

DISCERNING REALISM

In part because of this debate over birth control and authority, the renewal of moral theology continued. Attention turned to just how we go about making moral decisions. To many scholars, pastors, and ordinary decision makers, the pre-Vatican II style of strict obedience to law was not sufficient. Experience indicated that sometimes the letter of the law oppresses the spirit or simply cannot deal with the complexity of a particular case. Moreover, human dignity is more fully realized by a mature engagement in searching for the truth and coming to a decision—and not by just following a law.

The Roman Catholic tradition has held that morality is based on reality. Recent renewal has returned to the heart of this tradition, emphasizing that after careful discernment the individual must decide, but always in the context of the community's wisdom and with an understanding of what is really happening—not what one would like to happen. Actions have real meanings and consequences.

Returning again to our opening scene in the high school: the case discussed involved an elderly man who killed his ailing wife. The realism of Catholic morality demands that we discover and name what is actually happening, in this case the taking of life. Neither a sincere intention nor just calling this action "an act of mercy" can make it so. Of course, intentions and circumstances and consequences must also be included in the evaluation, but we must begin with accurately describing the action. Please note: our Catholic tradition has justified the taking of life in some situations (for example, self-defense), but in our case holds that sickness and pain are *not* sufficient reasons to take life. "Mercy-killing" (euthanasia) is not justified.

WHY, WHAT, HOW

Renewal and debate have given new insight into the why, what, and how of Catholic morality.

Why: The person's relationship with God, as expressed by Jesus' own example and in other great stories of the Bible, is the heart of morality. To live the moral life is to respond in love to God's call and graciousness in our lives. Sin is the breaking of this relationship.

What: Scripture also helps us to appreciate the specific content of the moral life. Jesus' teachings, for example, the good Samaritan story (Luke 10:30–37) and the Last Judgment scene (Matthew 25:31–46), remind us of our responsibilities for other people. His Sermon on the Mount (Matthew 5:1–7:29) gives us a challenging ideal to live by. The Ten Commandments, the wisdom of the prophets, and other parts of the Hebrew Scriptures provide important guidance. Insights from philosophy and the sciences, of course, are also helpful.

How: Mature moral decision making demands careful reflection and honesty and courage. Searching for the truth in a particular situation, listening to the wisdom of authority, and praying for insight mean hard work and a willingness to discern and decide. At the end of this appendix, we will see what this renewed why, what, and how of Catholic morality would mean for the persons in our opening scenes—and for all of us!

THE CATECHISM

The publication of the *Catechism of the Catholic Church* created quite a stir in our Church. The book quickly became a bestseller. Many people immediately turned to the section on morality, perhaps looking for the secure answers of the pre-Vatican II morality, perhaps hoping for expressions of the recent renewal. They found both.

The *Catechism of the Catholic Church*, as a summary of church teachings, in fact embodies both positive and negative aspects of Catholic moral theology. The *Catechism* follows the renewal of Vatican II by placing its whole discussion of the moral life under the title of "Life in Christ" and by rooting its view of humanity in Scripture. However, it follows the pattern of the earlier catechism (based on the Council of Trent, 1545–1563) by listing specific actions under the structure of the Ten Commandments rather than, for example, the Sermon on the Mount. The catechism seemed to ignore its own insight, "The Beatitudes are at the heart of Jesus' preaching" (1716), and so did not follow through on the mystery of Christ as the center of this long section of the text (2052–2557). Similar inconsistencies are found throughout the section, especially in those areas in which the older natural law approach is favored over the Vatican II emphasis on the whole person understood in historical context.

Nevertheless, the *Catechism* provides a summary of the official teaching on many of today's tough issues: genetic engineering, the death penalty, violence of all kinds, world economy, women's issues, AIDS, euthanasia, etc.

SOCIETY'S INFLUENCE

What has happened to Catholic morality? We have seen how Vatican II led to a profound renewal. Still, one other major influence on Catholic morality deserves attention. To appreciate what has happened to Catholic morality we must understand not only the internal dynamics of renewal and debate but also the external pressure of life in a particular culture. Here we will focus on our American life, with its technological advances and with its deeply rooted materialism and individualism.

Jesus did not have to worry about test-tube babies, genetic engineering, or respirators and other life-prolonging equipment. We do. Scientific and technological advances have clearly improved life, but they have also raised profound questions and challenges. Moral theology has had to respond to these amazing changes and to search for the right thing to do in such new circumstances. Clearly one significant insight from all this is the absolute necessity of accurate knowledge—and so the need to consult experts of all types when dealing with such complicated issues.

Of much greater importance for our reflections on Catholic morality, however, is the influence of the materialism and individualism of our culture. The significance of this point simply cannot be overstated. Even as we try to live according to the Gospel, we are constantly bombarded by TV, movies, music, and advertising—many of which communicate a very different set of values. Think of your favorite radio or TV programs and ask what messages about the moral life are *really* communicated in them.

We may not be aware of how profoundly our morality is shaped by our culture. Most of us spend many more hours each week watching TV than going to church or reading and studying religious books. Our life in a consumer society is judged by the clothes we wear, the cars we drive, the electronic "toys" we possess. Success, pleasure, power are most important. Looking out for #1—whether the self or one's country—is the basic message, whether presented subtly or not so subtly.

This emphasis on the individual and individual rights pervades our contemporary society and naturally influences us. It shapes our morality, almost unconsciously. The messages sound like this: "No one can tell me what's right or wrong." "Each person must decide for himself or herself." "If it feels good, do it!" The teenagers in our opening scene used these very words, even though they were in their eleventh year of Catholic education. Instead of carefully considering the moral implications of the action itself, this type of thinking, which is called relativism, holds that the individual's sincere intention is enough to make the action morally right or wrong. Pope John Paul II presented a thorough critique of relativism in his encyclical *The Splendor of Truth* (1993).

What has happened to Catholic morality? In our culture, it has often been overshadowed or even distorted by the dominant morality of the American way of life. We may not even be aware of how our social, economic, and political systems contradict the Gospel. We value things over persons, too easily turn to violence in place of peacemaking, stress retaliation rather than compassion.

CHALLENGE AND CHOICE

Let's return to our opening scenes and see what the why, what, and how of a renewed Catholic morality would mean for the teenagers and the older woman. We realize that the teenagers are at an age of seeking independence and identity. Still, their responses reveal a value system formed by modern media, not the Gospel. Perhaps they are open enough to hear the challenge of recognizing that religion does have something to contribute to decisions about life and death, of realizing that good intentions alone do not determine morality. All this will take time and experience. During this time, if they are lucky, friends, family, teachers will plant seeds of the Gospel vision. They might not turn to a renewed Catholic morality until they are jarred by some tragic life experience or until they have children of their own.

The older woman also needs to be open. She has already experienced much change in her practice of the Catholic religion. But, yes, still more is asked. The safe pre-Vatican II morality finally is not sufficient for an adult in our world. Her goodwill in attending the adult-ed class must spill over into a willingness to consider the depths of the moral life, the moral ambiguities present in our everyday world, the demands of a justice inspired by faith.

And you? The renewal and challenges of Catholic morality undoubtedly touch your life also. To appreciate the implications of this renewal, let's summarize several key points:

- *Morality is rooted in the life of Christ and all of Scripture.* Relationship with God is the very center of morality. Jesus' own love of God and faithfulness to his call offers us the perfect model and inspiration. Our relationship with God needs to be nourished not only by personal prayer but also by participating in a church community with a vibrant sacramental life and with a committed concern for others, especially the poor.

- *Morality is based on reality.* Our Catholic tradition challenges the individualism and relativism of our culture and urges us to search for the truth about moral decisions. With humility we recognize our need to consult many and varied wisdom sources as we form our consciences. With trust in our goodness and God's graciousness, we accept the responsibility to discern and decide and act—and so contribute to the flourishing of all creation.

- *Morality is rooted in social solidarity.* We all are God's daughters and sons. Every person is created in God's image, and so we respect the human dignity of all and care for all. Such a conviction often leads to a countercultural stance, with the consistent ethic of life guiding our political, social, and economic decisions. As faithful disciples and involved citizens, we must speak and act concerning welfare and immigration, sexism and racism, abortion and health care, euthanasia and the death penalty, genocide and trade agreements, and many other urgent issues.

Catholic morality has experienced a profound and rich renewal, inviting all of us into deeper love, trust, discernment, and dedicated action in our day-to-day lives. Catholic morality is also threatened by rigidity and the fear of change and especially by the materialism and relativism of our culture. The choice of value systems is yours. In his encyclical *The Gospel of Life*, Pope John Paul II dramatically describes this choice as a choice between a "culture of life" and a "culture of death." Choose life!